Italian
HOME COOKING

*Italian family recipes; passed down
from generation to generation.*

BY DR. DUANE LUND

Italian
HOME COOKING

First Printing 2009

Printed in the United States of America
by
Lund S&R Publications
Staples, Minnesota 56479

ISBN-13: 978-0-9740821-6-5
ISBN-10: 0-9740821-6-3

Dedication

To the second, third and fourth Italian-American generations who live on the Minnesota Iron Range who have so faithfully preserved the recipes and food preparation techniques brought to this country by their ancestors.

Table of Contents

Table of Contents

Chapter IV - Side Dishes

Chapter V - Main Dishes

Table of Contents

Chapter VI - Desserts

CHAPTER I

Toasted Almond Hors d' oeuvres

Ingredients to serve six:

6 cups whole almonds - blanched (but may have skins on)
2 T sugar
1 t salt
4 T extra-virgin olive oil
2 t crushed red pepper flakes

Combine the olive oil and red pepper flakes in a skillet and sauté over medium heat two or three minutes. Do not let boil. Stir constantly.

Transfer oil and pepper flakes to a bowl. Stir in the sugar and salt. Add the almonds and stir until well-coated.

Arrange the almonds on a flat baking pan - not touching. Bake in a pre-heated oven (medium) for 15 minutes - stirring a couple of times.

Hors d'oeuvres for six to eight:

2 cups green olives, pitted (may be stuffed)
2 cups ripe olives, pitted
4 cloves garlic, minced
zest from one orange - sliced thin
juice from one orange
2 bay leaves
2 basil leaves
6 T extra-virgin olive oil
1 pound cheese of your choosing - cut into half-inch squares
2 cups almonds, toasted

Combine olives, garlic, zest, orange juice, olive oil, bay leaves and basil leaves.
Toss and stir for several minutes. Refrigerate for at least six hours, stirring occasionally.

Serve cold or return to room temperature - your choice. Throw away basil and bay leaves and stir in cheese
cubes. Stir in almonds or scatter on top - your choice.

Antipasti

Marinated Olives Hors d'oeuvres

Ingredients to serve six:

4 cups assorted olives, pitted (may be whole, halved, or sliced)
1/2 cup extra-virgin olive oil
the juice of one lemon
1/2 T pepper flakes, crushed
2 T fresh basil, chopped or torn into small pieces

Combine the olive oil, lemon juice and red pepper flakes in a skillet. Cook just briefly until the oil just starts to boil - only a minute or two - stirring all the while.

Remove from the stove and stir in the basil and olives, making sure they are all well-coated.

Let cool to room temperature and serve. (May be kept refrigerated a day or two in a sealed jar.)

Green Dipping Sauce

Ingredients to serve six:

2 cups green olives with pimento stuffing
3 cloves garlic, minced
1 cup fresh parsley
2 ribs celery, chopped
1 cup mint leaves
juice of 1 lemon
1/2 cup cheese of your choosing - shredded (Parmesan works well.)

Using a food processor with a steel blade, blend until well mixed. Do not blend beyond the "chunky" stage.

A great dip for crackers, toast, vegetables, etc.

Antipasti

Green Sauce #2

Ingredients for four to six as a dip or spread or for seasoning:

1 cup extra-virgin olive oil
2/3 cup torn or chopped basil
1/4 cup chopped parsley
1/4 cup mint leaves
2 cloves garlic, minced
juice and grated zest of one lemon
1/2 t each of salt and pepper

Combine ingredients in a food processor with a steel blade. Add olive oil slowly, stopping when you have a fairly thick paste.

For an entirely different taste, try adding mayonnaise - tasting as you go.

Bruschetta Appetizer

Ingredients to serve four:

4 slices Italian (or French) bread - a "generous" half-inch thick
1 large tomato, topped, seeded and chopped (fairly fine)
2 T extra-virgin olive oil
3 T basil, torn or cut fine
1 clove garlic, minced
1/4 t each salt and pepper
mozzarella cheese, sliced thin, enough slices to cover bread

Place bread slices on a baking sheet. Brush bread with olive oil. Combine all other ingredients except cheese. Ladle over bread slices; spread to cover each slice. Top each slice of bread with cheese.

Bake in a pre-heated 350 degree oven until cheese melts. (About 10 minutes)

Cut each slice in half so that it is easier to handle.

Antipasti

Party Toasts (Brushetta #2)

Ingredients for eight slices of Italian bread, cut diagonally into half-inch thick slices:

2 tomatoes, chopped
6 green onions, chopped (use white parts only)
1 cup black olives, pitted and sliced
1 T capers
1 T minced garlic
3 T olive oil (in 3 parts)
2 T lemon juice
1 T chopped fresh oregano or basil or parsley
2/3 cup grated parmesan cheese

Make a paste by combining and blending the olives, 1 T olive oil, capers, lemon juice and garlic. Combine chopped tomatoes, onion, herbs and 1 T olive oil (use a spoon).

Brush both sides of bread slices with olive oil and toast in a 400 degree oven. Spread the paste on each slice of toast. Top with tomato mixture. Sprinkle with a little parmesan.

Return to the oven just long enough for the cheese to melt.

Tomato, Onion and Garlic Bruschetta #3

Ingredients to serve four:

1 loaf Italian (or similar) bread
4 tomatoes
2 cloves garlic, minced
1 large purple (red) onion, broken into rings
salt and pepper
3 T extra-virgin olive oil

Slice loaf of bread horizontally, end to end. Slice tomatoes and then cut slices into quarters. Mince garlic cloves. Combine topping ingredients.

Brush bread halves with olive oil and then brown in the oven under the broiler. Watch carefully; do not let burn. Spread topping evenly over bread. Cut into eight serving size pieces.

Antipasti

Tomato – Cheese Bruschetta #4

Ingredients to serve eight:

8 slices French or Italian bread, one inch thick
2/3 cup extra-virgin olive oil, divided
4 tomatoes, chopped
2 cloves garlic, minced
1 small onion, minced
4 T basil, chopped
2 t oregano
1/2 t each salt and pepper
1/3 cup mozzarella cheese

Place slices of bread on a baking sheet. Brush tops with half the olive oil. Bake in a pre-heated 350 degree oven 10 minutes or until brown.

Meanwhile, combine remaining olive oil with tomatoes, garlic, onion, basil, oregano, salt and pepper. Spread on the bread. Sprinkle with the cheese.

Cut each slice into two pieces to more easily handle. Serve immediately.

Fresh Tomato Bruschetta #5

Ingredients to serve four:

4 slices French or Italian bread, 1/2 inch thick
2 T virgin olive oil
2/3 cup chopped tomatoes (cherry or larger)
3 T chopped basil
4 T shredded mozzarella cheese (or your favorite)
4 green onions, chopped, both white and green parts

Brush bread slices with olive oil. Place under broiler until light brown.

Combine other ingredients and spoon over toasted bread slices. Cut each slice in half - lengthwise.

Antipasti

Mushroom Bread Spread

Ingredients for 8 slices Italian or French bread:

1 pound fresh mushrooms of your choosing, sliced
1/2 cup extra-virgin olive oil
8 slices bread
1 cup chopped parsley
1 cup cut or torn basil leaves
2 cloves garlic, minced
1/2 t each salt and pepper
2/3 cup grated cheese of your choosing (Parmesan works well)

Cover the sliced mushrooms with water in a sauce pan. Barely bring to a boil, then remove from heat and let sit until tender (15 to 20 minutes). Discard water.

Using a food processor, combine 1/2 of the olive oil, mushrooms, parsley, basil and garlic. Process until the mushrooms are well chopped. Stir-in the grated cheese.

Arrange the bread on a baking sheet. Brush each with the remaining half of the olive oil. Bake in a pre-heated 350 degree oven until bread starts to get brown and crisp. Spread equal portions of the mixture you have prepared onto the bread and serve.

Cheesy Bread Sticks

Ingredients for 20 - 24 bread sticks:

sheets of pasta (refrigerated bread stick dough is available in most supermarkets.)
2 T olive oil
1 cup grated cheese of your choosing (could use two varieties)
salt

Refrigerated bread stick dough usually comes in perforated rectangles about 8 inches long. If you use this type of pasta, separate the rectangles and then cut them in two lengthwise. If you make your own pasta, roll into thin sheets and then cut into pieces about 8 inches long and 1 1/2 inches wide.

Sprinkle each sheet with olive oil and grated cheese. With your fingers, roll them into sticks with the cheese inside. Sprinkle with salt.

Bake in a pre-heated 350 degree oven on a baking sheet until a golden brown - about 12 to 15 minutes.

Antipasti

Easter Bread

Ingredients:

3 cups all purpose flour
1/2 cup sugar
2/3 cup warm milk
2 t dry yeast
2 T warm water
3 T butter, softened
3 eggs, beaten
1 T anise seed
2 T poppy seeds

Dissolve yeast in warm water. Blend together and knead all ingredients except the poppy seeds. When the dough reaches a sticky consistency, place in a greased bowl. Turn to coat. Place in a warm location and cover with dish cloth. Let rise until volume doubles (about 1 1/2 hours).

Knead dough down. Divide into six equal portions. Roll each portion into a rope - about 15 inches long. Braid 3 of the ropes together. Braid the remaining 3 ropes together, thus forming two loaves. Place the two loaves on a greased cookie sheet; cover with the towel, place in a warm location; let rise until size doubles (no more than 1 hour). Brush with oil or egg. Sprinkle with poppy seeds. Bake in a pre-heated medium oven, about 350 degrees, until a golden brown (about 20-25 minutes).

Rolls with Cheese and Garlic Topping

Ingredients for about 20 rolls:

6 cups all purpose flour
2 cups warm water
1 1/2 T dry yeast
2 T sugar
1 T salt

For topping:

2 garlic cloves, diced
3 cups Parmesan cheese, shredded
2/3 cup extra-virgin olive oil
1/2 t oregano

Using a large bowl, add warm water and sprinkle with yeast and sugar. Let stand 10 minutes. Add 2 cups of flour and wisk until smooth. Stir in the remaining flour, about a half-cup at a time, with a wooden spoon. Dump dough onto a floured surface and knead until smooth - not sticky. Add a little more flour if necessary, a T spoon full at a time. Turn into a greased bowl, turning once to grease all surfaces. Cover with plastic and let rise until triple in size (about 2 hours).

Divide dough into rolls - about 3 inches - and place on greased cookie sheet. Cover with sheet of light plastic and let rise until double in size (about 30 minutes).

While oven pre-heats to 400 degrees, combine topping ingredients. Spread topping over each roll. Bake 20 minutes or until golden.

Tomato-Cheese Sandwich

Ingredients for one sandwich:

2 slices Italian or French bread (at least 1/2 inch thick)
2 slices mozzarella cheese (1/2 inch thick and large enough to cover a slice of bread)
2 or 3 slices of tomato (enough slices to cover a slice of bread)
basil leaves - enough to cover a slice of bread
salt and pepper - sprinkle lightly
3 T extra-virgin olive oil

Combine all ingredients into a sandwich and brush both sides of the sandwich with the olive oil.

Place on a grill or under a broiler, turning when first side is a golden brown and the cheese has melted. (Brown both sides)

Turkey or Chicken Panini

Ingredients to make four sandwiches:

8 slices of turkey or chicken breasts (about 1/2 inch thick and large enough to cover a slice of bread).
1/2 cup chopped and toasted walnuts or pecans
8 slices Italian bread (French will work)
2/3 cup bruschetta topper from grocer's refrigerated case
mayonnaise
lettuce leaves
olive oil

Spread mayonnaise on 4 slices of bread and bruschetta topper on 4 slices. Assemble sandwiches and brush with olive oil.

Place in a hot skillet and brown sandwiches on both sides (may use grill or place under broiler).

Antipasti

Open-face Egg Sandwich

Ingredients for one sandwich:

1 slice Italian or French bread, one inch thick
2 eggs (If the slice of bread is not large enough for two eggs, use just one)
salt and pepper
4 T extra-virgin olive oil
garlic salt
2 t grated Parmesan cheese
4 T crushed tomatoes

Place two T olive oil in a skillet and fry the eggs on both sides. (If you like a runny yolk, just fry on one side.) Sprinkle eggs with salt and pepper.

Meanwhile toast the slice of bread until well browned.

Brush the top of the toast with the remaining olive oil. Sprinkle with crushed tomatoes. Sprinkle lightly with garlic salt. Sprinkle with Parmesan cheese. Top with eggs.

CHAPTER II

SOUPS

Tomato Soup

Ingredients to serve six to eight:

2 14 oz. cns diced or crushed tomatoes (preferably Italian style)
2 10 oz. cns chicken broth or chicken soup
1 14 oz. cn Navy Beans
1 green bell pepper, seeded and cut into strips
4 T parsley, fresh clipped or flakes
1 t oregano (dried)
2 cloves garlic, minced
1 t salt
1 t black pepper (ground)

Blend all ingredients except parsley (in a blender). Place in a soup pot and bring to a boil. Reduce heat and simmer for twenty minutes. Serve in bowls sprinkled with parsley.

Chilled Tomato Soup

Ingredients to serve four:

2 T extra-virgin olive oil
2 cloves garlic, minced
4 t chopped onion
3 pounds tomatoes
2 cups seasoned croutons
1/3 cup basil leaves, torn into small pieces
2 T sugar

Sauté the garlic and onions a couple of minutes or until onion is just translucent.

Combine all ingredients and use a food processor to make an "almost smooth" soup.

Refrigerate and chill several hours before serving.

Soups

Tomato - Basil - Bread Soup

Ingredients to serve four:

2 - 14 1/2 oz cns. crushed tomatoes (preferably Italian style)
1 cup water
1/2 cup chopped basil
1 t oregano
3 slices Italian or French bread, one inch thick, cut into 1 inch cubes, toasted
1/2 t each salt and pepper
2 cloves garlic, minced
4 T olive oil, divided

Brush bread slices with olive oil. Place under broiler until they turn brown. Cut into one inch cubes.

Sauté the minced garlic in the remaining olive oil for one minute or until it just starts to turn brown.

Meanwhile, combine the crushed tomatoes, basil, oregano, salt and pepper in a sauce pan and bring to a boil. Reduce heat to low and stir in garlic and bread cubes.

(Italian seasonings flavored croutons may be substituted for the bread or combined with it.)

Minestrone (vegetable soup)

Ingredients to serve six:

2 cloves garlic, minced
1 medium onion, chopped
2 ribs celery, sliced thin
1 pound Italians sausage (bulk) or sausages, cut bite-size
4 T extra-virgin olive oil
1 large (or two small) potatoes, peeled and chunked
1 carrot, scraped and sliced
1 - 14 1/2 oz. cn. diced tomatoes (preferably Italian style)
1 medium zucchini - sliced
1 t basil, dried
1 t oregano, dried
1/2 t each salt and pepper
1/4 t red pepper flakes
2 T catsup
5 cups water

Sauté the garlic*, celery, onion and sausage in the olive oil until onion is translucent.

Transfer to a soup kettle and add all other ingredients. Bring to a boil, reduce heat to simmer and cook about 20 minutes or until vegetables are tender. Serve hot.

*Add garlic last; don't let it turn brown.

Soups

Zucchini Soup

Ingredients to serve six:

2 pounds zucchini, peel two of the zucchini; chop these squash and remaining squash into quarter inch chunks (save peelings)
4 cloves garlic, minced
1 onion, peeled and chopped
4 T extra-virgin olive oil
5 cups water
1/2 cup basil, packed
1/2 t each salt and pepper

Sauté onion and garlic in the olive oil until onion is translucent. Add four cups of water, the chopped zucchini and the salt and pepper and bring to a boil, then reduce heat to simmer and cook 15 minutes or until chunks are soft (stirring every few minutes).

Let cool, then purée the soup plus the basil in a blender in three batches. Meanwhile, cut the zucchini peelings into narrow strips and then cook these strips in the remaining cup of water until tender.

Re-heat soup until piping hot. Serve with strips of zucchini floating on top of each bowl.

Fish Soup with Tomatoes

Ingredients to serve four:

1 1/2 pounds fish fillets, skinned and de-boned (most any kind of fish works well)
1 30 - 43 oz. can diced or crushed tomatoes (preferably Italian) or 3 - 14 1/2 oz. cans
1 onion, diced
3 cloves garlic, minced
2 ribs celery, cut thin
1 carrot, scraped and cut thin
1 cup white Zinfandel wine
1 1/2 cups water
1/2 cup parsley, chopped for garnish
salt and pepper
3 T extra-virgin olive oil

Sprinkle fillets lightly with salt and pepper. Cut into bite-size pieces.

Sauté the onion and garlic in the olive oil until onion is translucent and the garlic just starts to turn brown.

In a soup kettle, combine first 8 ingredients. Cook over medium heat until vegetables are done, then add fish and cook another 10 - 12 minutes or until fish flakes easily with a fork.

Serve in bowls with parsley scattered on top as a garnish.

Soups

Fish Soup with Vegetables and Seasoned Croutons or Toast

Ingredients to serve six:

3 pounds fish fillets (Now that my Iron Range friends have learned to de-bone northern pike,
   that is their favorite)
1 zucchini (sliced thin in cross-sections)
2 carrots (scraped and sliced thin)
4 ribs celery, cut thin
6 large tomatoes, topped, seeded and chopped
4 cloves garlic, minced
1 onion, chopped
1 cup chopped cabbage
6 T extra-virgin olive oil
2 cups white wine
2 cups water
1/2 t each salt and pepper

Cut de-boned fish into bite size chunks. In a large, non-stick skillet, sauté the zucchini, carrots, celery, cabbage, salt and pepper in the olive oil over medium heat for 10 minutes or until all vegetables are done. Add the onion and garlic the last minute. Stir occasionally.

Add the tomatoes, fish, water and wine and continue cooking until fish flakes easily (about 10 minutes). If you prefer to serve the soup with toast, cut a loaf of Italian or French bread into half inch slices. Toast on each side under your broiler, then brush with olive oil (one side) and sprinkle lightly with garlic salt. Cut the slices in half and invite your guests to dip the toast in their soup. If you prefer, forget the toast; just sprinkle seasoned croutons liberally on the surface of the soup.

Seafood Soup

Ingredients for eight servings:

2 pounds mussels or scallops or boneless fish or combinations thereof
1 lg can (32 oz.) plum tomatoes, chopped (save juice)
1 large onion, broken into rings
3 T minced garlic
4 cups water
2 cups white wine
3 T chopped oregano
1/2 t Tabasco or other hot sauce
2 T olive oil
1 cup parsley, fresh, chopped

If you use mussels, clean, de-beard and cook in boiling water until they open. Sauté the onion rings in the oil until translucent; do not burn.

Combine the following in a large soup kettle: water, wine, seafood, tomatoes, tomato liquid from the can, garlic, oregano and Tabasco. Bring to a boil and then reduce heat and simmer 15 minutes or until the seafood is done.

Serve with garlic toast.

CHAPTER III

SALADS

Insalata Caprese (Caprese Salad) *

Ingredients to feed four:

3 vine-ripe tomatoes, 1/4 inch thick slices
1 pound fresh mozzarella, 1/4 inch thick slices
20 - 30 leaves (about one bunch) fresh basil
Extra-virgin olive oil, for drizzling
coarse salt and pepper

Layer alternating slices of tomatoes and mozzarella, adding a basil leaf between each, on a large, shallow platter. Drizzle the salad with extra-virgin olive oil and season with salt and pepper to taste.

*Courtesy Judy Jenkins, Staples, MN and Lisa Kruchten, Naples, Fla.

White Bean Salad with Canned Salmon or Tuna

Ingredients to serve four:

Lettuce leaves to line four salad bowls
1 - 7 or 8 oz. cn. salmon or tuna, chopped bite-size
1/2 cup zucchini, chopped
2 carrots, scraped and sliced thin
2 ribs celery, sliced thin
1 sweet red pepper, seeded and cut into narrow strips
1 - 15 or 16 oz. cn. white beans, drained
1/3 cup green or black olives, sliced

Dressing ingredients:

1/3 cup extra-virgin olive oil
juice of one lemon
zest from one lemon
3 T wine (or vinegar)
1/2 t each salt and pepper

for garnish:

1/3 cup chopped parsley

Line salad bowls with lettuce. Combine salad ingredients and toss. Shake dressing ingredients in a sealed jar. Toss with salad ingredients and distribute among four salad bowls.

Garnish with parsley.

Salads

Pasta Salad with Smoked Fish

Ingredients for six servings:

1/2 package pasta of your choice - 8 oz. (suggest penne or bow tie)
2 cups flaked smoked fish (salmon is my favorite)
12 green onions, sliced (both green and white parts)
2 cups thinly sliced zucchini or eggplant or asparagus or combination thereof
3 T extra-virgin olive oil
1 sweet red pepper, seeded and cut into narrow strips
1 sweet green pepper, seeded and cut into narrow strips

Ingredients for dressing:

1/2 cup extra-virgin olive oil
juice of one lemon
zest from one lemon
2 T dill weed
1/2 t each of salt and pepper

Sauté the zucchini or other vegetables in the 3 T of olive oil. Meanwhile, cook the pasta according to the directions on the package. Drain and let cool.

Combine the dressing ingredients by shaking them vigorously in a covered jar. Combine all salad ingredients and toss - several times - with the dressing until well coated. Refrigerate at least two hours. Toss again before serving.

Tomato and Cheese Salad

Ingredients to serve six:

6 tomatoes, topped, seeded and cut into bite-size pieces
2 cucumbers, peeled, seeded and cut into thin slices
1 sweet, green pepper, seeded and cut into narrow strips
1 onion, peeled and chopped
3 cloves garlic, minced
1 cup black olives, halved or sliced
6 basil leaves, cut or torn into small pieces
3 T parsley, chopped (for garnish)
8 ounces cheese of your choice, cut into quarter inch cubes (mozzarella works well)
1 T olive oil
Ingredients for dressing:
1 1/2 cup extra-virgin olive oil
4 T wine (or substitute vinegar)
1/2 t each salt, pepper and sugar

Sauté the garlic briefly in 1 T olive oil, then combine with all of the salad ingredients in the first list except the parsley.

Shake the dressing ingredients in a tightly closed container, then toss vigorously with the other salad ingredients and top each serving with parsley.

Salads

Tomato and Cheese Salad #2

Ingredients to serve six:

juice of one lemon
1/2 cup extra-virgin olive oil
salt and pepper
2 pounds of tomatoes (may be a variety) sliced or cut into wedges (bite-size)
1/2 pound mozzarella cheese, sliced and cut bite-size
8 fresh basil leaves torn or cut thin

Prepare a dressing by whisking together the lemon juice, olive oil and 1/2 t salt and 1/2 t pepper.

Arrange tomatoes and cheese pieces on a platter. Drizzle the dressing over-all. Sprinkle with basil leaves.

Tomato - Garden Vegetable Salad

Ingredients to serve four:

1 1/2 pounds of a variety of tomatoes (red, yellow, cherry size, etc.) sliced or cut into wedges.
2 medium carrots, scraped and sliced thin
2 ribs celery, sliced thin
1/2 cup grated cheese of your choice
4 T extra-virgin olive oil or liquid Italian dressing
4 T wine or wine vinegar of your choosing
4 T fresh parsley flakes
1/2 t each salt and pepper

Shake wine, olive oil (or Italian dressing), salt and pepper in a covered jar.

Distribute tomato slices or wedges, carrots and celery on four plates. Drizzle wine-olive oil mixture over vegetables. Scatter cheese and parsley over each serving.

Salads

Tortellini Salad

Ingredients to serve four:

1 pkg. Cheese-filled tortellini (refrigerated)
3 T sliced green onions (including both green and white parts)
1 rib celery, thin slices
1 carrot, sliced thin (raw or cooked)
1 cup green beans, sliced and cooked

Dressing ingredients:

1/3 cup extra-virgin olive oil
1/3 cup red wine (or red wine vinegar)
1/2 t oregano (dried)
1/4 t garlic salt

Cook tortellini according to directions on the package. Drain. Cook beans (carrot optional).

Meanwhile, place dressing ingredients in a lidded jar and shake well.

Place all salad ingredients in a bowl and gently stir-in dressing.

Chicken Salad with Tortellini

Ingredients to serve four to six:

1 package (20 oz.) frozen tortellini with cheese, thawed
1 1/2 cups cooked chicken meat (a great way to use leftovers) cut bite-size
4 ribs celery, sliced thin
6 strips bacon, broiled and broken into small pieces
1 cn. kidney beans, 15 1/2 oz., drained (white, if available)
1 cup Italian dressing or liquid dressing of your choosing

Prepare tortellini according to directions on the package. Drain and cool.

Add all other ingredients and stir together.

Refrigerate at least two hours before serving.

Salads

Chicken Salad with Ham

Ingredients to serve six to eight:

3 pounds left-over (cooked) chicken, cut into bite-size chunks
1 pound pre-cooked ham, sliced thin and cut into strips (bite-size)
lettuce leaves - enough to line each bowl
6 T extra-virgin olive oil
3 lemons, zest and juice of
2 green onions, both green and white parts, chopped
2 zucchini, peeled and chopped
2 sweet peppers (any color or mixed) seeded and cut into strips
2 carrots, scraped and sliced thin
1/2 pound blue cheese, crumbled
1/2 t each salt and pepper

Combine chicken, green onions, zucchini, sweet peppers, carrots and cheese.

Make dressing by combining olive oil, lemon juice, lemon peel, salt and pepper.

Line individual bowls with lettuce leaves. Spoon equal portions of salad mix into the bowls. Sprinkle with dressing. Top each bowl with ham strips.

Panzanella (bread and vegetable salad)

Ingredients to serve six:

5 slices Italian or french bread, one inch thick (cut into one inch cubes)
1 cup green beans, cut into inch and one-half lengths
1 cup asparagus, cut into one and one half inch lengths
1 cup zucchini, sliced thin
1/2 cup extra-virgin olive oil, divided
12 cherry tomatoes, sliced in half
3 cloves garlic, minced
1 sweet onion, sliced thin and broken into rings
1/2 cup green olives, pitted and sliced in two
1/2 cup black olives, pitted and sliced in two
basil leaves sliced into 12 strips
1/2 cup wine vinegar or Italian dressing

Brush one side of bread slices and place under broiler until golden brown. Turn over and repeat. Let cool and cut into one inch cubes.

Place remaining olive oil in a skillet and sauté the asparagus, green beans and zucchini until soft. Add garlic for one additional minute, stirring all the while.

Place all ingredients in a large bowl and toss.

Salads

Shrimp Salad

Ingredients to serve four:

1 pound shrimp, peeled and deveined
4 tomatoes, topped, seeded and chopped
1 medium sweet green pepper, seeded and cut into strips
1 medium red pepper, seeded and cut into strips
1 sweet onion, peeled and chopped or broken into rings
1 cucumber, peeled and cut thin
2 cups seasoned croutons

Ingredients for dressing:

1/2 cup extra-virgin olive oil
1/2 cup red wine or wine vinegar
1 clove garlic, minced

Place shrimp in lightly salted water, bring to a boil; remove from heat; let stand a minute or two or until shrimp is opaque.

Combine salad ingredients and place equal portions in four bowls.

Combine dressing ingredients and sprinkle over four bowls.

Pasta Salad with Shrimp

Ingredients to serve six:

2/3 of a 16 oz. Package of pasta of your choosing (small sea shell variety is appropriate.)
24 large pre-cooked shrimp
6 green onions, chopped - both white and green parts
1 pkg. frozen peas, thawed
2 ribs celery, cut into thin cross-sections
1 small jar pimientos, drained
2/3 cup white tartar sauce
1/2 t salt

Prepare pasta according to directions on the package. Drain and rinse with cold water through a sieve.

Combine all ingredients in a large bowl and toss until shrimp and pasta are well-coated.

Cover with plastic and refrigerate at least two hours before serving.

Salads

Crispy Bread Salad

Ingredients to serve four:

4 cups Italian bread cut into 1/2 inch cubes
1 rib celery, sliced thin
1/2 medium size cucumber, seeded and sliced
1/2 cup green onion sliced (including green portion)
1 carrot, sliced thin and cut into half-slices
1/3 cup black olives, pitted and sliced
1/3 cup green olives, pitted and sliced
1/2 cup parsley, cut into 2 - 3 inch pieces
1/2 cup extra-virgin olive oil
1/3 cup red wine (optional)

Bake bread cubes in pre-heated 350 degree oven on a pan. Bake 20 minutes, stirring bread cubes several times until a golden brown. Cool completely.

Combine all ingredients, topping with the parsley.

A Christmas Salad

Traditionally, the salad is made and then refrigerated up to 3 days before Christmas Eve. Ingredients for eight servings:

8 anchovy fillets
1/2 cup sliced black olives
1 head cauliflower
1/3 cup olive oil
1 T vinegar (preferably white wine)
3 T minced marjoram (or other favorite herb)
1/3 cup capers
1 cup pickled red peppers, sliced
water to cover cauliflower plus 1 t salt for the water

Break the cauliflower head into smaller pieces. Cover with water (salted) and bring to a boil; reduce heat and cook for about 4 minutes until cauliflower is tender but still crisp. Drain and let dry.

Toss with all other ingredients. Refrigerate (up to 3 days).

Salads

Pasta Fruit Salad

Ingredients to serve eight:

1 16 oz. package of shell (or similar) pasta
1 cup orange juice
2 cups yogurt (plain)
2 small cans mandarin orange slices, drained
1 pear, cored, peeled and diced
2 cups seedless grapes, halved
1 large or 2 small apples (hard variety), cored and diced
2/3 cup shelled walnuts, chopped
2 ribs celery, chopped coarse

Prepare the pasta; let cool. Combine all ingredients, tossing gently.

Bell Pepper Salad

Ingredients to serve four:

4 bell peppers - may be of assorted colors
1/2 cup olives, pitted - may be a combination of black and green. May be sliced.
4 T extra-virgin olive oil
3 garlic cloves, minced
salt and pepper (1/2 t each)
2 T chopped parsley
2 T torn basil leaves

Bake the peppers in a 300 degree oven (on a baking sheet) for 20 minutes - turning occasionally. When they are done they will start to blister and turn brown. Let cool, then seed and cut into strips (bite-size).

Combine all ingredients in a bowl and toss until well coated with olive oil. May serve at room temperature or after refrigeration.

Salads

CHAPTER IV

SIDE DISHES

Creamy Bow Tie Pasta

Ingredients to serve six:

1 16 oz. pkg. bow tie pasta
1 cup chicken broth or soup
1 onion, peeled and minced
3 cloves garlic, minced
2 T extra-virgin olive oil
6 basil leaves cut or torn into small pieces
1/2 t each salt and pepper
1 cup whipping cream

Prepare pasta according to directions on the package. Meanwhile, sauté the minced garlic and onion in the olive oil for a couple of minutes or until onion is translucent (add the garlic at the end; don't let brown).

Add the broth, salt and pepper and bring to a boil, then reduce heat and cook for 10 minutes, stirring frequently. Add the cream; continue stirring until sauce is reduced to a little more than half.

Drain pasta and combine with sauce - also stir in basil.

Squash Side Dish

Ingredients to serve four:

4 cups of sliced squash (one variety or two or three kinds. Zucchini blends well with most any kind of
   squash. If rind is heavy, remove before slicing. Cut thin slices or bite-size chunks.)
3 cloves garlic, minced
3 T extra-virgin olive oil
6 basil leaves, torn into small pieces
1 cup mozzarella cheese, grated

In a heavy, non-stick skillet, sauté the squash pieces in the olive oil over medium heat for about 5 minutes
or until squash is soft, stirring all the time. Add the garlic and stir for another minute.

Remove from heat and stir in basil and cheese. Serve hot. Have butter available as an option for your guests.

Side Dishes

Orecchiette with Vegetables and Pine Nuts

Ingredients for four side dishes:

8 oz. orecchiette pasta (funnel-shaped)
1 cup broccoli florets
1 cup asparagus, cut bite-size
1/2 cup pine nuts, toasted (or substitute a nut of your choosing, chopped)
5 T extra-virgin olive oil
3 cloves garlic, minced
4 T Parmesan cheese, grated

Dressing ingredients:

1/2 cup extra-virgin olive oil
juice of one lemon
1 t dill weed
4 T wine or vinegar

Prepare the pasta according to directions on the package. Meanwhile, sauté the asparagus and broccoli in the olive oil until soft. Add minced garlic and stir for another minute.

Shake the dressing ingredients in a sealed jar. Toss with vegetables. Drain pasta and combine with vegetables. Toss some more. Divide into four warm bowls. Sprinkle each bowl with nuts.

Potatoes with Herbs on the Grill

Yes! Italians do eat potatoes!

Ingredients to serve four:

Four potatoes, quartered (If large, cut into more sections. If skins are edible, leave them on.)
3 cloves garlic, minced
4 basil leaves, cut or torn into small pieces
4 thyme leaves, chopped fine
1/3 cup chopped parsley
1/2 t each salt and pepper
3 T extra-virgin olive oil

Combine the seasonings. Brush the potato sections with the olive oil. Roll in the bowl of seasonings.

Place potatoes between two sheets of heavy foil. Place on top of medium-hot grill. Cook for 20 minutes, then turn packet and cook for another ten minutes or until potatoes are tender.

Serve with left-over olive oil.

Side Dishes

Mashed Potatoes with Cream Cheese and Herbs

Ingredients to serve six:

6 large potatoes, peeled and quartered
6 oz. cream cheese, softened
1 stick (quarter pound) butter (softened)
1/2 t each salt and pepper
6 basil leaves, cut or torn into small pieces
6 t parsley flakes (for garnish)
1/3 cup milk

Boil the potato chunks in a sauce pan 15 minutes or until done.

Drain potatoes and place in a large bowl and mash until smooth. Add all other ingredients except parsley and beat until well blended. Use parsley for garnish when serving.

Potato Noodles (Gnocchi)

Ingredients to serve six:

8 medium size potatoes, peeled and quartered
1 cup flour
two eggs
1/2 t each salt and pepper
1 stick (quarter pound) butter, melted
6 T basil leaves, torn or cut into small pieces (may substitute your favorite seasoning)
4 T Parmesan cheese, grated
water

Cover potato chunks with water (in a large saucepan). Boil for 15 minutes or until soft. Drain. Press the potatoes through a ricer or mash. Make a hole in the middle of the mound of potatoes. Combine the salt, pepper and eggs and beat until smooth. Sprinkle 2 T flour over the potatoes and pour the egg mixture into the hole. Stir with a fork until blended and smooth.

Sprinkle a surface with flour. Knead the potato mixture a dozen or more times or until it forms a dough. Cut the dough into four parts and roll each part until it forms a half inch thick rope. Cut each rope into 3/4 inch sections. Flatten each section with a fork.

In a large saucepan, bring water to a boil and cook the noodles in batches for about a minute. As they float to the surface, remove them with a slotted spoon. In a separate saucepan, melt the butter and then mix in the basil, then add the noodles. Stir gently until coated. Remove and sprinkle with cheese.

Spicy Spuds
Some like them hot!

Ingredients to serve four:

4 large, red potatoes, skins on, cut into bite-size chunks (about 4 pounds)
1/2 cup extra-virgin olive oil
3 cloves garlic, minced
1 onion, minced
1 T (level) red pepper flakes (Adjust amount to how hot you want the potatoes.)
1/2 T salt

Combine the last four ingredients in a bowl. Brush the potato chunks with olive oil. Toss a few chunks at a time in the spices. Arrange potatoes on a greased cookie sheet - sides not touching.

Bake in a 350 degree oven for about 45 minutes or until potatoes can be easily pierced with a fork.

Drizzle leftover olive oil over potatoes before serving. (Or guests may dip chunks in saucers of olive oil)

Potato Frittata

Ingredients to serve 6:

3 large white potatoes, peeled and thinly sliced
6 eggs (large)
3 T virgin olive oil
1 onion, chopped
2 cloves garlic, minced
1/3 cup heavy cream
salt and pepper (a dash of each)
1 T each chopped parsley and basil (fresh)
1/3 cup grated Parmesan cheese (or other cheese of your choosing)

In a 10 inch oven-safe skillet, sauté the onion and garlic in the olive oil until the onion is translucent. Add the sliced potatoes, salt and pepper and continue to cook over low heat until potatoes are tender (about 15 minutes).

Blend the eggs and cream and stir into the ingredients in the skillet and continue to cook a couple of minutes. Meanwhile, start the broiler in your oven. Scatter the Parmesan over the contents of the skillet and place under the broiler until a golden brown.

Slide the skillet contents onto a dinner plate and sprinkle parsley and basil over top. Cut into six pie-shaped wedges and serve.

Side Dishes

Seasoned Potatoes

Ingredients for eight servings:

4 large potatoes, sliced through lengthwise
2 T olive oil, divided into 2 portions
1/2 T Italian seasoning
1/4 t salt
1/2 T pepper, freshly ground
1/2 t paprika

Make several half-inch cuts with a knife in the cut surface of each potato. Brush oil on the potato surfaces. Brush oil on a cookie or baking sheet. Place potatoes, cut side down, on the sheet. Bake 45 minutes at 350°.

Mix 1 T oil with the seasonings. Turn potatoes over with a spatula and brush with seasoned oil. Return to oven, this time with cut side up, and bake another 45 minutes until done.

Tomato Ravioli

Ingredients to serve eight as a side dish or four as a main dish:

1 1/2 pounds frozen, cheese-filled ravioli
eight tomatoes, seeded and quartered
5 cloves garlic, minced
1 onion, peeled and minced
1 cup shredded cheese of your choosing (Parmesan works well)
8 basil leaves, torn or cut into narrow strips
2 cups greens of your choosing - lettuce works well
1/2 t each salt and pepper
4 T virgin olive oil

Prepare the cheese-filled ravioli according to directions on the package. While the ravioli is cooking, combine all ingredients in a large bowl except the garlic and onion.

In a large skillet, sauté the onion and garlic* for a minute or until onion is translucent. Stir in the contents of the salad bowl and cook over medium heat for seven or eight minutes, stirring occasionally.

Place cooked ravioli on each plate and spoon contents of the skillet over the ravioli.

*Add the garlic last; do not let brown.

Side Dishes

Tomatoes Stuffed with Left-over Turkey

Ingredients for side-dishes to serve six:

6 large, ripe tomatoes
3 cups cooked turkey (or chicken), ground or chopped fine
1 can (12 oz.) mixed vegetables, drained
2 cloves garlic, minced
1 onion, minced
3 T extra-virgin olive oil
2 T torn or chopped cilantro
2 T torn or cut basil
1 cup shredded cheese of your choosing (Parmesan or cheddar both work well)

Cut tops off tomatoes. Scoop out insides (chop insides and save).

Sauté in olive oil in a large skillet garlic and onion for a couple of minutes until onion turns translucent and garlic starts to brown. Combine turkey, chopped tomatoes, mixed vegetables and cheese and add to the skillet. Continue cooking until hot, stirring slowly.

Meanwhile, bake tomato shells in a pre-heated 300 degree oven for five minutes.

Stuff tomatoes and sprinkle with basil and cilantro. Serve hot.

Fried Green Tomatoes

I'm not sure this is an authentic Italian recipe but I am sure it is a great way to use up some of those green tomatoes in your garden at the end of the growing season!

Ingredients to serve four:

6 green tomatoes sliced about a quarter inch thick

3 eggs

1/2 cup water

2/3 cup cornmeal

1/2 cup flour

1/2 cup Parmesan cheese, grated

1/2 cup extra-virgin olive oil

1/2 t oregano

1 T basil, chopped

1 t garlic salt

1/4 t crushed red pepper flakes

Whisk together the eggs and water in a small bowl. Combine the cornmeal, flour, cheese and seasonings in another bowl. Dip each tomato slice in the egg mixture and then in the second bowl.

Sauté the tomato slices in the olive oil, frying 4 or 5 minutes on each side until a golden brown. Let dry on paper towel but serve them warm.

Side Dishes

Dandelion Greens

When Italians migrated to this country, one of the foods they missed was cicoria (a kind of chicory). With a little experimentation, however, they found that dandelion greens made an excellent substitute.

Ingredients:

1 gallon dandelion greens (discard tough lower stems) cut with a scissors into 2 to 3 inch pieces.

3 cloves garlic, mashed

1/3 t red pepper flakes

1/3 cup extra virgin olive oil

1/2 t salt

Put greens in a large pot and cover with water. Sprinkle with 2 t salt; bring to a boil; cook 8 to 10 minutes or until greens are tender. Drain through a colander and rinse thoroughly with cold water.

In a skillet, add olive oil and warm over medium heat for 4 or 5 minutes. Add red pepper flakes and mashed garlic. Sauté until a light brown. Add greens and sprinkle with 1/2 t salt. Stir gently as you continue the cooking process for another 5 minutes or until greens are well covered with oil and other ingredients.

May be served hot or cold.

Ratatouille *

Ingredients to serve six as a side dish:

1 eggplant (about one pound) peeled and cut into bite-size cubes
1 or more zucchini (about one pound total) peeled and cut into bite-size cubes
4 T extra-virgin olive oil
3 large tomatoes, peeled, seeded and chopped
2 red onions, sliced and broken into circles
2 red or green bell peppers, cut into thin strips about 2 inches long
3 cloves garlic, minced
1/2 t each salt and pepper
1/3 cup chopped basil
1 t thyme
1 bay leaf

In a large skillet, sauté the eggplant and zucchini pieces until tender (don't over-cook) - about 10 minutes. Remove eggplant and zucchini with a slotted spoon and set aside. In the same pan, reduce heat and sauté the onion rings two or three minutes, then add garlic and continue cooking another minute. Remove with a slotted spoon and set aside.

In the same pan, add the tomatoes and the remaining ingredients and cook another five minutes. Then, return the set-asides to the skillet, cover, and continue to cook over medium heat another 10 minutes or until eggplant and zucchini are tender, but check every few minutes so as to not over-cook. Remove bay leaf before serving.

*Courtesy Jerry Mevissen, Sebeka, MN

Summer Vegetable Side Dish

Ingredients to serve four:

eggplant - 8 half-inch slices
zucchini - 8 cross-cut half-inch slices
tomatoes - 12 cherry size tomatoes, halved or 4 medium tomatoes, quartered
2 cloves garlic, minced
1 onion, sweet variety, broken into rings
1 sweet green pepper, seeded and cut into strips
4 T extra-virgin olive oil
4 T red wine
4 T flour
1/2 t each salt and pepper - combine with flour

Dust the eggplant and zucchini with flour and salt and pepper mixture and sauté (both sides) in the olive oil. (About six minutes per side). Sauté the garlic along with the vegetables the last minute.

Optional: sauté tomatoes along with the eggplant and zucchini the last six minutes (or serve raw).

Divide the vegetables on four plates and scatter with onion rings and pepper strips and sprinkle with wine. Serve hot.

Zucchini with Wine

Ingredients to serve four as a side dish:

4 large zucchini, sliced into half-inch sections
4 T extra-virgin olive oil
1/2 cup red wine
2 T chopped parsley

Sauté the zucchini in the olive oil in a large skillet. Brown sections on each side. Add wine and cook until wine evaporates, turning each section over once.

Sprinkle with parsley flakes as a garnish.

Side Dishes

Ingredients to serve four:

3 medium zucchini, sliced cross-wise (should equal 3 to 4 cups)
2 cloves garlic, minced
1 medium onion, chopped
4 T extra-virgin olive oil
2 medium tomatoes, topped, seeded and diced (not small)
1 T basil, torn or cut into small pieces
1/2 t oregano (dried)
1 1/2 cups shredded cheese of your choice (Parmesan, cheddar or mozzarella all work well)
1/2 t each of salt and pepper

Sauté the zucchini in the olive oil until soft. Add onion and garlic and continue a couple more minutes.

Add all other ingredients and continue cooking and stirring until cheese has melted. Serve hot.

Mediterranean 3 Bean Salad

Ingredients to serve four (main dish servings):

3 cns. (about 16 oz. each) assorted beans
4 ribs celery, sliced extra thin
1 carrot, scraped and sliced extra thin
3 green onions, sliced, both white and green parts
1 head lettuce
16 anchovies* (preferably smoked) head, tail, bones and fins removed, cut bite-size
4 T extra-virgin olive oil
1 lemon, juice of

Combine all ingredients except the lettuce. Make beds of lettuce leaves on four plates. Distribute equal portions of the salad ingredients on the beds of lettuce.

*Minnesotans living in the northern part of the state often use smoked herring from Lake Superior.

Side Dishes

Chicken Broth with Eggs

Ingredients for eight servings:

7 cups chicken broth
3 large eggs (4 small)
4 T chopped parsley
4 T grated parmesan cheese
salt and pepper to taste

Heat the broth until it simmers (bubbly, but not boiling). Add salt and pepper to taste.

Meanwhile, beat together the eggs, cheese and parsley flakes (until frothy). Slowly pour the egg mixture into the hot broth, stirring as it is added. Let cook without stirring no more than 1 minute (eggs should set).

Serve with croutons or toast.

Linguini with Ham

Ingredients to serve eight as a side dish or four as a main dish.

1 16 oz. package or box linguini
2 pounds cooked ham, cut in bite-size chunks or strips (your choice)
1 package frozen peas (about 4 cups)
1/2 cup whipping cream
2 cups shredded Parmesan cheese
4 T extra-virgin olive oil

Prepare the linguini according to directions on the package.

Meanwhile, in a large, non-stick skillet, sauté the ham and peas.

When linguini is done, drain and combine with ham, peas, cheese and cream. Serve hot.

Side Dishes

CHAPTER V

MAIN DISHES

Hot Sauce with a Touch of Brandy

Ingredients to serve four:

1 16 oz pkg. of pasta of your choosing
2 - 14 1/2 oz. cns. crushed tomatoes (preferably Italian style)
4 T extra-virgin olive oil
2 onions (medium) chopped
3 cloves garlic, minced
1 rib celery, sliced very thin
6 basil leaves, torn or cut into thin strips
1/2 t each of salt and pepper
2/3 cup brandy (room temperature) Vodka also works well

Sauté the onion, garlic and celery in the olive oil until the onion is translucent.

Add the tomatoes, basil, salt and pepper to the skillet and cook until piping hot.

Meanwhile, prepare the pasta according to directions on the package and drain. Divide into four portions. Add the brandy to the sauce and pour equally onto the portions of pasta.

Quick and Easy Tomato Sauce

For use with one pound of your favorite pasta or in other Italian recipes.

Ingredients:

8 average size tomatoes, chopped
3 cloves garlic, minced
4 T extra-virgin olive oil
1/2 t each salt and pepper

herbs to be added - some or all, your choice

basil leaves (6-10) in strips, torn or chopped
3 t oregano
3 T parsley, chopped
2 T chopped rosemary

Saute the garlic in the olive oil for one minute. Stirring all the while. Add the chopped tomatoes, salt and pepper. Cook over medium heat 10 - 12 minutes.

Stir in the herbs.

Main Dishes

Spaghetti / Meat Sauce #1

Ingredients to serve four:

1 pound lean ground beef
1 - 16 oz. box spaghetti (or other favorite pasta)
4 T grated Parmesan cheese
2 #2 cns. crushed or diced tomatoes or 1 cn. each (preferably Italian style)
3 cloves garlic - minced
1 t oregano (dried)
1 medium onion, chopped
1/2 cup extra-virgin olive oil

Sauté the ground beef in the olive oil, along with the garlic, oregano and onion.

When the hamburger is well-browned, stir in the tomatoes and continue cooking until hot. Meanwhile, cook the spaghetti according to the directions on the box.

Portion the pasta onto each plate, add the sauce to each serving, sprinkle each serving with the grated Parmesan cheese.

Spaghetti / Meat Sauce #2

Ingredients to serve four:

1 pound Italian sausage (if bulk sausage is not available, buy links and remove casings)
1 - 16 oz. box spaghetti (or other favorite pasta)
2 T extra-virgin olive oil
1 onion, diced
1 - 28 oz. cn. diced or crushed tomatoes (preferably Italian style)
2 garlic cloves, minced
1/2 cup fresh basil leaves, cut into strips
2/3 cup Parmesan cheese, grated

Add the oil to a skillet and sauté onion and garlic a couple of minutes. Crumble the sausage and add to the skillet, stirring gently until sausage is well browned.

Add tomatoes and continue to cook 10 minutes, stirring occasionally. Meanwhile, prepare the pasta according to directions on the package.

Portion the spaghetti onto four plates. Pour equal portions of the sauce over the pasta. Scatter the basil strips over each portion. Sprinkle the Parmesan cheese over each portion.

Main Dishes

Meatballs with Spaghetti

Ingredients to serve four:

1 - 16 oz. box or package spaghetti or other favorite pasta
1 pound ground beef
1/2 cup dried bread crumbs
1 onion, minced
1/4 cup chopped basil
2 eggs
2 T milk
1 cup grated cheese of your choosing (Parmesan works well)
1/2 t each of salt and pepper
4 T extra-virgin olive oil
2 - 14 1/2 oz. cns. crushed tomatoes (preferably Italian style)

Combine the ground beef, bread crumbs, onion, basil, eggs, milk, salt and pepper and half of the grated cheese. Roll into balls about the diameter of a half dollar.

Add the olive oil to a skillet and brown the meatballs over medium heat, turning every two or three minutes until well browned. Add the crushed tomatoes to the skillet and the rest of the grated cheese and continue to cook until piping hot.

Meanwhile, prepare the pasta according to directions on the package and drain. Divide the pasta onto four plates and top with equal portions of the sauce and meatballs.

Spaghetti with Anchovy Sauce

Ingredients to serve four:

1 box (16 oz.) Spaghetti or other favorite pasta
1 small can (2 oz.) Anchovies (chopped)
2 cups bread crumbs
1/2 cup extra-virgin olive oil
1 cup red onions, sliced thin
3 T chopped dill or parsley
1/2 t red pepper flakes
1/2 t each of salt and pepper

Place half of the oil in a skillet and sauté the bread crumbs until brown (stir constantly). Remove crumbs to paper towel.

Add remaining oil to skillet and sauté onions until translucent. Add chopped anchovies and mash with a fork into the onions. Meanwhile, cook spaghetti according to directions. Drain but save 1/2cup water.

Stir together reserved water, pepper flakes, salt, pepper and half the bread crumbs into the anchovy sauce. Portion the spaghetti onto four plates. Add sauce to each serving. Sprinkle each serving with remaining bread crumbs and chopped dill or parsley.

Main Dishes

Spaghetti Puttanesca

Ingredients to serve four:

1 - 16 oz. box spaghetti (thick works best - most authentic)
1 cn. diced or crushed tomatoes - use Italian if available (14 1/2 oz.)
1/2 cup extra-virgin olive oil
2 garlic cloves, minced
1/2 cup pitted and sliced olives (black or green)
2 small cns. (2 oz.) Anchovy fillets (chopped)
4 t capers
3 T parsley flakes or chopped fresh

Place olive oil in a skillet. Sauté garlic until brown. Add tomatoes and cook over medium heat about 10 minutes. Add capers, chopped anchovies and olives. Continue to cook another couple of minutes.

In the meantime, prepare the spaghetti according to directions on the package. Drain pasta; mix well with sauce; sprinkle with parsley.

Spaghetti Sauce with Bacon

Ingredients to serve four:

1 - 16 oz. box or package of spaghetti or pasta of your choice
8 slices of thick bacon, cut into bite-size chunks
3 T extra-virgin olive oil
1 onion, chopped fine
3 cloves garlic, minced
2 - 14 1/2 oz.cns. crushed tomatoes (Italian style)
1/2 cup grated Parmesan cheese
salt and pepper (1/2 t of each)
optional: 1/2 t crushed red pepper flakes

Sauté the bacon pieces in a skillet, stirring so as not to burn but should be brown. Set aside.

Discard bacon grease. Add olive oil to skillet. Saute onion and garlic until onion is translucent. Add all other ingredients to skillet (including bacon) and cook over medium heat until piping hot.

Meanwhile, prepare pasta according to directions on the package.

Main Dishes

Ingredients to serve four:

1 box or 16 oz. package spaghetti
2 - 14 1/2 oz. cns. diced or crushed tomatoes, preferably Italian style (or use fresh tomatoes)
3 garlic cloves, minced
3 stalks celery, sliced very thin
2 carrots, scraped and sliced very thin
3 T extra-virgin olive oil
salt and pepper, 1/2 t each
2 basil leaves, torn thin

In a skillet, sauté the onions, garlic, celery, and carrots until the onion is translucent (about 10 minutes). Add the basil. Sprinkle with the salt and pepper, stirring well.

Add the tomatoes and continue to cook until the sauce starts to thicken.

Meanwhile, prepare the spaghetti according to directions on the package and drain. Divide the spaghetti on four dinner plates and top with equal portions of the sauce.

Spaghetti Sauce Without Meat - Recipe #2

Ingredients to serve four:

1 box or 16 oz. package spaghetti or other favorite pasta
1 pound fresh tomatoes
4 T extra-virgin olive oil
3 garlic cloves, minced
1 onion, chopped fine
3 T mozzarella cheese, small cubes - about 1/3 inch
3 T finely chopped Parmesan cheese
4 T torn basil leaves
salt and pepper

Sauté the onion and garlic in the olive oil in a skillet.

Using a food processor, pulse the tomatoes, mozzarella cheese, onion, garlic and basil. Stir in the Parmesan cheese and about 1/2 t each of salt and pepper.

Meanwhile, prepare the pasta according to the directions on the package. Drain and divide onto four plates. Top with the sauce.

Main Dishes

Spaghetti Sauce #3 with Lots of Herbs

Ingredients to serve four:

1 - 16 oz. package spaghetti or pasta of your choosing
3 T extra-virgin olive oil
3 cloves garlic, minced
3 T minced onion
3 pounds fresh tomatoes, chopped fine (save the juice)
salt and pepper
your favorite herbs

Sauté the garlic and onion in the olive oil until the onion is translucent (a couple of minutes). Add the diced tomatoes and juice to the pan along with 1/2 t each of salt and pepper. Cook until piping hot. Stir frequently.

Meanwhile, prepare the spaghetti according to the directions on the package.

Remove the sauce from the heat and stir in your favorite herbs. Possibilities:
1/3 cup torn basil leaves
1 T chopped rosemary leaves
1 T chopped sage leaves
2 T chopped parsley

You may also add 1/2 cup or more of grated cheese of your choice (Parmesan works well).

Distribute the pasta equally to four bowls or plates and then spoon on sauce.

Meatless Spaghetti Sauce #4

Ingredients to serve four:

1 - 16 oz. box or package of spaghetti (or other favorite pasta)
2 - 14 1/2 oz. cns. crushed or diced tomatoes (preferably Italian)
3 cloves garlic, minced or run through a garlic press
1/2 cup pitted and sliced olives of your choice
2 T anchovy paste or chopped, anchovies
1/2 t red pepper flakes
3 T extra-virgin olive oil
1/2 cup basil, sliced or chopped

Cook spaghetti according to directions on the box or package.

Sauté garlic, anchovy paste or chopped anchovies in the olive oil for three minutes. Add tomatoes and olives and continue cooking until hot.

Drain spaghetti and add to the pot and gently stir until pasta is well-coated.

Serve on four plates. Sprinkle with basil.

Main Dishes

Ingredients to serve four:

Use any of the previous four recipes, but add 2 cups of olives (one or several varieties) pitted and sliced or halved. If you like it hot, stir in 1 t crushed red pepper flakes.

"Some Like it Really Hot"

Pasta Sauce Without Meat – Recipe #6

Ingredients to serve four:

1 box or 16 oz. package pasta of your choosing
2 - 14 1/2 oz. cns. crushed tomatoes, preferably Italian style
3 T extra-virgin olive oil
1 onion, minced
3 t garlic cloves, minced
2/3 cup olives, pitted and halved or sliced
1/2 t salt
1/2 t pepper
1 t crushed red pepper flakes (or substitute minced jalapeno pepper - I know they are Mexican -but I love their flavor!)

Sauté the minced onion and garlic in the olive oil in a skillet until the onion is translucent.

Add all other ingredients and continue to cook over medium heat until piping hot.

Meanwhile, prepare the pasta according to the directions on the package.

Main Dishes

Pasta with Mushroom Sauce

Ingredients to serve four:

1 pound pasta of your choosing; for a main course I prefer tortellini
1 cup fresh mushrooms, sliced (may use dried mushrooms - 1/2 cup)
1 stick butter (1/4 pound) melted
4 T chopped thyme
4 T chopped basil
8 green onions, chopped, both green and white parts
1 cup grated Parmesan cheese
1/2 cup heavy cream
1/2 t each salt and pepper

Prepare tortellini according to directions on the package.

Sauté chopped onions, mushrooms, salt, pepper and herbs in the melted butter until the onions are brown and tender. Add cream and continue to cook. Stir until well blended.

Drain pasta, add sauce and Parmesan cheese and toss until well coated.

Pasta with a Touch of Mustard

Ingredients to serve four:

16 oz. pasta of your choosing
3 T extra-virgin olive oil
12 Italian sausages, spicy variety, casings removed and meat crumbled
1/2 cup whipping cream
2/3 cup white wine
4 T mustard
1/2 cup basil, cut or torn into thin strips
2 T oregano
1/2 t crushed red pepper

Prepare pasta according to directions on the package.

Sauté the sausage in the olive oil in a non-stick skillet (about 5 minutes or until brown). Add all other ingredients to the skillet and cook for another 5 minutes, stirring all the while.

Drain pasta and add to the skillet; toss to coat.

Main Dishes

Spaghetti Sauce with a Bite *

Ingredients:

3 cans Hunts Tomato Sauce
1 can tomato paste
1/4 cup olive oil
medium onion chopped
3 cloves garlic chopped
1 cup water
3 large bay leaves
4-5 shakes of oregano
1 tsp crushed red pepper
1 tlbs sugar
dash of pepper
shot of red wine

Sauté the onions and garlic in the olive oil. Add remaining ingredients and simmer for one hour. Liberally sprinkle with Parmesan cheese and simmer for an additional hour.

Use immediately, or freeze for future use.

*Courtesy Beth Chandler, Lake on the Hills, IL

Vodka Sauce *

Ingredients:

2 large cans of crushed tomatoes (unseasoned)
1/3 cup vodka
1 stick of butter
1 pint heavy whipping cream
1/4 cup olive oil
1/2 cup romano cheese
1 small onion
salt and pepper

Mince the small onion using a food processor, if you don't have one make sure you chop the onion into small pieces. Add a stick of butter, olive oil and minced onions into the pot, cook on medium heat for a few minutes. Add 1/3 cup of vodka and continue to cook for 5 minutes, lower the heat if needed. You do not want to brown the onions, just sauté.

Add the two cans of crushed tomatoes to the pot and cook for 45 minutes. Add salt and pepper to taste. Add pint of heavy whipping cream after sauce cooks for 45 minutes. Wait 15 minutes and add 1/2 cup of romano cheese. Cook for about 5 minutes more.

*Courtesy Beth Chandler, Lake on the Hills, IL

Main Dishes

Spaghetti with Bacon and Eggs

Ingredients to serve four:

1 pound box or package of spaghetti
4 eggs
1/2 pound thick bacon cut into bite-size pieces (about 1 inch by 1/2 inch)
1 cup grated cheese (cheddar works well)
1/2 t each salt and pepper
3 T olive oil

Prepare the spaghetti according to the directions on the package.

Meanwhile, fry the bacon in the olive oil until crisp. Remove bacon from pan and set aside. Save olive oil and bacon fat. Combine the eggs, fat, cheese, bacon bits, salt and pepper (in a serving bowl).

Drain the spaghetti and stir it into the other ingredients until well coated. Serve hot.

Chicken and Asparagus Alfredo

Ingredients to serve four:

1 - 16 oz. package linguine
1 cup asparagus, cut into bite-size pieces (broccoli may be substituted)
2 pounds skinless, boneless chicken breasts cut into bite-size pieces
3 T extra-virgin olive oil
1 cn. cream of mushroom soup
1 cn. milk
1/2 t black pepper
2/3 cup Parmesan cheese, grated

Prepare linguini according to directions on the box. Add asparagus pieces the last five minutes.

Add oil to skillet and sauté chicken pieces until done, stirring and turning frequently.

Drain linguini and place all ingredients except cheese - including pasta - in the skillet. Cook over medium heat, stirring occasionally, until bubbly.

Sprinkle Parmesan over each serving.

Main Dishes

Chicken and Eggplant on the Grill*

Ingredients to serve six:

12 chicken thighs, skinned and deboned, and cut in half
1 or 2 eggplants - 24 2 inch cubes
6 tomatoes - about 4 inches in diameter, cut in half
3 cloves garlic, minced
1/2 cup extra-virgin olive oil
2 t rosemary, dried
1 t oregano
1 T basil, chopped fine

Make a marinade (in a bowl) of the garlic, olive oil, rosemary, oregano and basil. Coat each chicken thigh half thoroughly in the marinade.

Using at least 6 skewers, load them alternately with pieces of chicken, egg plant and tomatoes.

Position the skewers about 4 inches above the heat source on an outdoor grill. Baste occasionally with the marinade. Turn skewers occasionally to insure even cooking. Should be done in 10 minutes or a little longer.

*Courtesy Jerry Mevissen, Sebeka, MN

Baked Tuscan Chicken *

Ingredients to serve four:

16 oz. fettuccine
4 chicken breast halves, skinned and de-boned
1 egg
2 cups water
4 T butter, melted
1 cup bread crumbs
4 T chopped basil
1/2 t lemon pepper
2 carrots, scraped and sliced
1 zucchini, peeled and sliced

Ingredients for sauce:

2 large tomatoes, chopped
3 T parsley, chopped
3 cloves garlic, minced
3 T extra-virgin olive oil

Prepare a sauce by combining the ingredients listed. Let stand while baking the chicken and cooking the pasta and vegetables. Combine egg and water in a bowl and beat until blended. In another dish, combine the bread crumbs, basil and lemon pepper. Dip each chicken breast in the egg-water mixture and then in the dish of bread crumbs, etc. Make sure both sides of the breast are well covered. Place the chicken in a baking dish and drizzle with the melted butter. Bake in a 350 degree oven 40 minutes or until cooked through.

Meanwhile, cook the pasta according to directions on the package. Add the carrots and zucchini and let cook with the pasta. Drain the pasta and vegetables and divide among four plates. Spoon equal portions of the sauce over each serving. Option: Sprinkle with grated Parmesan.

*Courtesy Jerry Mevissen, Sebeka, MN

Chicken with Risotto

Ingredients to serve four:

4 cups cooked chicken without skin or bones - cut bite-size (great use for leftovers)

1 cup risotto (saffron flavored rice) uncooked (if not available regular rice works well)

3 cups chicken broth or chicken soup

2 - 16 oz. cns. crushed or diced tomatoes (Italian style)

4 T virgin olive oil

3 cloves garlic, minced

1 onion, peeled and chopped

2 cups sliced mushrooms (or 1 cup sliced, canned mushrooms, drained)

4 T Parmesan cheese, grated (for garnish)

Sauté the mushrooms and onions in the olive oil for a couple of minutes or until onion is translucent. Add the garlic and cook and stir another minute.

Add all other ingredients (except the cheese) and cook until piping hot and rice is cooked, stirring regularly.

Serve in bowls with cheese sprinkled on top for garnish.

Chicken Thigh Pasta *

Ingredients to serve:

Cut 6 to 8 boneless, skinless chicken thighs into small pieces
Brown in olive oil and butter
Add one small onion, chopped
Add 1/2 t each basil, oregano and minced garlic
Add 1 - 15 oz. cn. basil, oregano and garlic tomatoes
Add 1 - 8 oz. cn. tomato sauce
1 - 7 oz. cn. Mushrooms (optional)
In a separate pan, cook your favorite pasta
Pour the chicken mixture over the pasta

* Courtesy Tom Honek, Staples, Minnesota

Main Dishes

Chicken Scaloppine

Ingredients to serve four:

8 chicken fillets - breast meat - skin removed
1/2 cup chicken broth or soup
4 T onion, minced
4 T melted butter
2 T Italian seasoning
1 t salt
1 t pepper
1 T extra-virgin olive oil
1 T lemon juice
1 large tomato, diced
2 cups sliced mushrooms
20 asparagus tips, blanched and cooled
1/2 cup shredded Parmesan cheese
1 cup all-purpose flour

Prepare asparagus ahead of time.

Slice chicken fillets 1/2 inch thick. In a zip-lock bag, place chicken, flour, salt, pepper and Italian seasoning. Shake well and lightly pound ingredients into chicken pieces.

Sauté chicken pieces on both sides in olive oil and melted butter. When chicken is done, add all remaining ingredients except the Parmesan cheese. Place chicken on serving plates and spoon sauce over each. Sprinkle Parmesan cheese over each serving.

Chicken and Pasta Casserole

A great recipe for left-over chicken.

Ingredients to serve four:

3 cups cooked chicken, cut into bite-size pieces
1 can cream of mushroom soup
2/3 cup milk
1/3 cup Parmesan cheese, grated
1/3 cup cheddar cheese, grated
2 cups pasta of your choosing, cooked
1 cup frozen mixed vegetables, thawed
1/2 t black pepper

Cook the pasta according to the recipe on the package.

Meanwhile, stir together all other ingredients except the cheddar cheese.

Combine the pasta and the other ingredients you have just combined and pour into an oven-safe casserole dish. Top with cheddar cheese and bake in a pre-heated 350 degree oven for thirty minutes.

Main Dishes

Tortellini with Ham and Chicken

Ingredients to serve 4 or 8 as a side dish:

16 oz. pkg. tortellini with cheese
1 cup cooked chicken, cut bite size (may substitute turkey)
1 cup cooked ham, cut bite size
1 cup mozzarella cheese, cubed bite size
1 cup frozen green peas, thawed
4 ribs celery, sliced thin
1/2 sweet green pepper, seeded and cut into narrow strips
1/3 cup chopped parsley
1/3 cup chopped basil
1 small onion, chopped
1/2 cup virgin olive oil
3 cloves garlic, minced
1/2 cup wine (may substitute vinegar)

Prepare the tortellini according to directions on the package.

Meanwhile, sauté the garlic in the olive oil in a large pan for one minute but not until garlic turns brown.

Add all ingredients (except tortellini) to the pan and cook over medium heat 10 minutes, stirring every couple of minutes. When contents are hot, drain the tortellini and add to the pan. Toss gently to coat.

Serve hot or let cool and refrigerate at least two hours.

Left-over Turkey with Tortellini

Ingredients to serve six:

4 cups left-over cooked turkey (or chicken)
1 pound frozen cheese tortellini (thawed) or other pasta (dried)
2 cloves minced garlic
2 T minced onion
2 T olive oil
1 small can sliced mushrooms, drained
1 can (11 oz.) cream of mushroom soup
1 can (11 oz.) chicken soup
1 box frozen vegetables, thawed
1 cup milk
1 cup shredded cheese of your choice (Parmesan and cheddar both work well - could use half of each)

Cook the pasta according to the directions on the package.

Meanwhile, sauté the onion and garlic in the olive oil a couple of minutes or until onion is translucent.

Add all ingredients (except the cheese) to the skillet and continue to cook until piping hot, stirring occasionally. Sprinkle cheese on top. Cover and continue cooking until cheese melts.

Main Dishes

Ground Turkey or Chicken Sauce Over Pasta

Ingredients to serve four:

1 - 16 oz. box pasta of your choosing
1 pound ground turkey or chicken (preferably dark meat) Iron rangers sometimes used grouse
3 T extra-virgin olive oil
1 onion, minced
3 cloves garlic, minced
2 - 14 1/2 oz. cns. crushed tomatoes (preferably Italian style)
1 carrot, scraped and minced
1 rib celery, cut extra thin
1/3 cup cut or torn basil leaves
1/4 cup chopped parsley
salt and pepper - 1/2 t each
1/3 cup cheese of your choice, grated
optional: 1/2 t crushed red pepper flakes

Add the oil to a skillet and sauté the onion and garlic over medium heat until onion is translucent but before the garlic* is brown. Add the carrot and celery and continue another 5 minutes. Add the ground poultry and continue cooking and stirring until meat is done.

Add all other ingredients and continue cooking and stirring until piping hot. Meanwhile, prepare the pasta according to the directions on the package.

*Add garlic later.

Chicken or Turkey Meatballs on Pasta

Ingredients to serve four:

1 - 16 oz. box or package spaghetti or pasta of your choosing
1 pound ground turkey or chicken (preferably dark meat)
1/3 cup dried bread crumbs
1 small onion, minced
1/4 cup chopped parsley
1/2 t each of salt and pepper
2 - 16 oz. cns. crushed or diced tomatoes (preferably Italian style)
4 T extra-virgin olive oil
1/3 cup torn basil leaves

Combine the ground poultry, bread crumbs, onion, garlic, salt and pepper. Roll into balls about the size of a half dollar. Add olive oil to a skillet and brown the meatballs, turning every few minutes until well browned.

Add the tomatoes, basil and parsley and cook until piping hot.

Meanwhile, prepare the pasta according to the directions on the package and drain. Divide the pasta onto four plates and top with the sauce and meatballs.

You may substitute beef or other red meat for the poultry.

Main Dishes

Hot Turkey Sausage with Penne Pasta

Ingredients to serve four:

1 1/2 pounds hot turkey sausages (casings removed)
1 pound penne pasta
3 T extra-virgin olive oil
1 cup endives (escarole)
2 tomatoes, topped, seeded, and cut into quarter inch chunks
3 cloves garlic, minced
1 onion, peeled and chopped
1 - 14 1/2 oz. cn. white beans
6 basil leaves, chopped
1 cup shredded cheese of your choosing
1/2 t each of salt and pepper

Prepare the pasta according to directions on the package.

Meanwhile, in a large skillet, sauté the greens, tomatoes, onion, garlic, sausage, salt and pepper in the olive oil over medium heat - for about 10 minutes or until sausage shows no pink. You may need to break apart the sausage with a spoon.

Drain the pasta, saving 1 cup of the liquid. Add the pasta, liquid and beans to the skillet and continue cooking and stirring for another 10 minutes.

Scatter cheese over each serving.

Chicken Cacciatore with Italian Sausages

Ingredients to serve four:

4 chicken thighs with drumsticks attached
1 pound Italian link sausages (mild or hot - your choice)
4 T extra-virgin olive oil
2 - 14 1/2 oz. cns. crushed or diced tomatoes (preferably Italian variety)
2/3 cup red wine
3 garlic cloves, minced
salt and pepper

Add 2 T oil to skillet and sauté and brown chicken and sausages over medium heat. Set aside.

Add remaining oil to skillet and sauté garlic a couple of minutes. Return chicken to skillet and let simmer over medium heat, turning so pieces do not burn (about 6 or 7 minutes).

Add all ingredients to skillet, salt and pepper lightly and let simmer (low heat) another 15 minutes. Cut sausages diagonally into thick, bite-size slices. Serve on a large platter or divide equally on four plates. Invite guests to add salt and/or pepper to taste.

Main Dishes

Strombolli *

Ingredients:

1 pkg dry yeast
1 cup luke warm water
1 tsp melted shortening or olive oil
1 tsp sugar
3 cups flour (any kind)
1 egg

Fillings:

1 pound or more pepperoni, sausage, mushrooms
1 pound or more mozzarella (may substitute summer sausage, provolone cheese, brocolli,
   cheddar cheese)

Mix yeast, water, shortening (oil) and sugar. Add flour - let set 5 minutes; mix; add flour and water as
needed to achieve texture of pizza dough.

Flour counter top. Shape out a little with hands - roll thin (like pizza dough). When done, put pepperoni,
cheese (whatever) in center. Cover filling in the shape of French bread.

Preheat oven to 400 degrees. Bake until golden brown - let cool. Slice into half inch servings -Serve.

Can be frozen in ziplock bags after being sliced. Cover with warmed rague sauce.

*Courtesy Tom Wolhowe, Staples, MN

Traditional Lasagna

Ingredients to serve four:

1 pkg. 16 oz. lasagna pasta
1 pound Italian sausages (hot or sweet), casings removed and contents crumbled
1 pound hamburger, crumbled
1 cup shredded cheese of your choosing (traditionally Ricotta)
1 cup Mozzarella cheese, shredded
4 T extra-virgin olive oil

Prepare pasta according to directions on the package. Let cool.

In a large, non-stick skillet, sauté the meat, separately, in the olive oil (until there is no pink showing).

Starting with one of the meats, layer the ingredients in a 9 x 12 lasagna pan. For example, a layer of hamburger, a layer of pasta, a layer of sausage meat, a layer of cheese, a layer of pasta, a layer of hamburger, etc. The last layer (top) should be Mozzarella.

Bake for 45 minutes in a pre-heated 375 degree oven (or until you can see the juices bubble).

Main Dishes

Quick Lasagna

Ingredients to serve six:

1 - 16 oz. pkg. lasagna pasta
4 T extra-virgin olive oil
1 pound ground beef (may substitute mixture of beef, pork and veal)
1/2 cup ricotta cheese
1/2 cup mozzarella, shredded
1/2 cup wine (preferably red)
1/2 cup basil, chopped
1/3 cup parsley, chopped
2 ribs celery, sliced thin
1 carrot, scraped and chopped
3 cloves garlic, minced
1/2 cup milk
2 cns. tomatoes, crushed or diced (preferably Italian style)

Prepare lasagna pasta according to directions on the package.

Meanwhile, in a large, non-stick skillet, add the olive oil and then sauté the hamburger, breaking it into small pieces. When pink color is no longer visible, add the wine, garlic, onion, carrot, celery, basil and parsley and continue to cook and stir for five more minutes. Then add the tomatoes and bring to a boil. Reduce heat and let simmer ten minutes. Stir in milk and cheese and let simmer another 5 minutes.

Drain pasta and add to the skillet. Toss until pasta is well-coated. Spoon mixture onto 6 plates.

Fettuccine Alfredo

Ingredients to serve four:

1 - 16 oz. pkg. fettuccine pasta
1/4 lb. (1 stick) butter, cut into small pieces and softened
1/3 cup of grated cheese of your choosing (traditionally Parmigano)
1 - 9 or 10 oz. cn. sliced, cooked mushrooms, drained
salt and pepper to taste

Prepare fettuccine according to directions on the package. Drain. Add butter, cheese, mushrooms, salt and pepper and toss until pasta is well-coated and cheese and butter are melted.

Main Dishes

Fettuccine Alfredo #2

Intended as a first course.

Ingredients to serve eight:

1 pound fettuccine
1 1/2 mushrooms, sliced (preferably morels)
3 T cognac
1 1/2 cups cream (traditionally heavy)
6 T butter, melted
1/3 cup grated parmesan cheese
1/2 t salt
1/2 t pepper
water to cook fettuccine

Combine 2 T of the melted butter, cognac, cream, salt and pepper. Bring to a boil; reduce heat to simmer; add mushrooms; cook 10 minutes or until the mushrooms are tender.

Meanwhile, cook the fettuccine in a pot of boiling water for about 3 or 4 minutes or until tender. Drain. Toss with the remaining melted butter. Add creamed mushroom mixture and toss.

Serve with grated parmesan.

Duck Ragu

Ingredients to serve four:

Two tame ducks or 3 wild mallards
Pasta of your choosing (16 oz.)
2 T extra-virgin olive oil
1 medium onion, chopped
2 garlic cloves, minced or squashed
1/2 cup red wine
1 cn. (14 1/2 oz.) diced tomatoes (preferably Italian style)
salt and pepper

Cut duck breasts from the carcass. Leave skin on. (Save legs and thighs for another meal). Rub salt and pepper into both sides of each breast. Sauté duck breasts (both sides) until brown. Remove from pan and set aside. Add onion and garlic to skillet and sauté until onion is done (translucent).

Return duck to skillet . Add wine and tomatoes. Simmer until duck is cooked-through. Skim off most of the fat on the surface. Remove duck and chop fine (with or without skin - your choice).

Meanwhile, prepare pasta according to directions on package. Drain pasta and toss with other ingredients.

Main Dishes

Penne Pasta with Tomatoes and Ripe Olives

Ingredients to serve four:

1 - 16 oz. package or box penne pasta (or pasta of your choosing)
2 cns. (14 1/2 oz.) diced tomatoes (preferably Italian style)
3 T extra-virgin olive oil
2/3 cup ripe olives, pitted and sliced
3 cloves garlic, minced
2 T capers
10 basil leaves, torn or sliced thin
1/2 t red pepper flakes

In the olive oil, sauté the garlic a couple of minutes. Add the capers and continue another minute or two. Add the tomatoes, red pepper flakes and olives and continue cooking until piping hot.

Meanwhile, prepare the pasta according to directions on the box and drain. Distribute the pasta on four plates and top with the sauce. Garnish with the basil.

Fresh Garden Peas, Green Onions and Pasta

Ingredients to serve four:

1 pound penne pasta or pasta of your choice
2 pounds fresh garden peas (no pods)
8 garden green onions, chopped - both green and white parts
4 garlic cloves, minced
4 T extra-virgin olive oil
1/2 t hot red pepper flakes
1/2 t each salt and pepper
1 cup grated cheese of your choosing
1 cup water
juice of one lemon

Prepare the pasta according to the directions on the package.

Meanwhile, sauté the garlic over low heat in the olive oil for just a couple of minutes. Add all other ingredients but start with only a half cup of water and then add as much of the rest of the cup as needed to give you a sauce that is not too watery.

Drain the pasta and divide among four plates and top with sauce.

Main Dishes

Tortellini with Nuts

Ingredients to serve four:

1 package cheese tortellini (16 oz.) from grocer's refrigerated display case
1/2 cup chopped nuts of your choosing (walnuts or pecans work well)
1 stick (quarter pound) butter - sliced thin
4 T spoons shredded Parmesan cheese
1/2 cup minced parsley
salt and pepper to taste

Prepare tortellini according to the directions on the box. Meanwhile, melt the butter. Stir together all ingredients except the Parmesan cheese - sprinkle this on top and serve while still hot.

Hot and Spicy Italian Skillet*

Ingredients:

2 lbs. Spicy Italian sausage
1 (28 oz.) can tomatoes
1 can or 1 pkg. frozen Italian green beans (substitute cut green beans)
2 cans garbanzo beans, drained
1 medium onion, chopped
1 green pepper, cut in julienne strips
1/2 tsp. ground cumin
1 clove garlic, minced
1 1/2 tsp. salt
1/2 tsp. Italian seasoning

In a covered large skillet over medium heat, cook sausage with 1/4 cup water for 5 minutes. Remove cover and brown sausage well. Add onion and garlic and fry until onion is translucent. Drain fat. Stir in tomatoes, Italian beans, garbanzo beans, green pepper and seasonings. Heat to boiling. Reduce heat to low. Cover and simmer 20 minutes. Serves 4-6

*Courtesy Jeanne Leifermann, Staples, MN

Main Dishes

Easy Camper's Skillet Lasagna *

Ingredients:

1 lb. ground beef
1 pkg. dry spaghetti sauce mix
1 (8 oz.) carton cottage cheese
2 c. (1/2 lb.) lasagna noodles
2 c. canned diced tomatoes, undrained
1 tsp. salt
1 1/2 tsp. parsley
1/2 c. water
1 c. mozzarella cheese, shredded

Brown meat. Sprinkle with 1/2 of the spaghetti sauce mix. In the same pan, spread cottage cheese in a layer over the meat. Spread noodles over the cottage cheese. Add remaining sauce mix, salt and parsley, sprinkling over the noodles. Add 1/2 of the mozzarella. Pour tomatoes and water over the mixture. Cover with frying pan cover or foil. Cook on low heat or over a low fire for 35 to 40 minutes or until noodles are cooked. Sprinkle remaining mozzarella on top. Cover until the cheese melts. Serves 4 to 6.

*Courtesy Jeanne Leifermann, Staples, MN

Jeanne's Meat and Pasta *

Ingredients:

4 Italian sausages, mild or hot
4 pork chops
4 chicken breast fillets
salt and pepper to season chops and fillets
1 lge. onion, chopped
2 cloves garlic, chopped
3 lge. cans tomato sauce
3 tsp. Italian seasoning
1 box spaghetti, angel hair pasta, or linguini

Brown meats in a large Dutch oven in a small amount of oil, seasoning with salt and pepper. Remove from pan. Sauté onion and garlic until onion is soft and translucent. Return meats to pan. Pour tomato sauce over the meats. Add Italian seasoning. Cover and simmer for 1 hour. Cook pasta according to package directions. Drain. Serve the meats and sauce over the hot pasta.

*Courtesy Jeanne Leifermann, Staples, MN

Main Dishes

Sauce for Steak

Ingredients for a sauce to enhance steaks for two:

Two steaks of your preference, prepared as you wish
4 T extra-virgin olive oil
2 garlic cloves, minced
1 onion, minced
1/2 t hot red pepper flakes
1/3 cup pitted and sliced black olives
1/3 cup pitted and sliced green olives (if stuffed with pimentos, leave them in)

Sauté the garlic, onion, pepper flakes and olives in the olive oil until the onion is translucent.

Pour the sauce over the steaks.

Seasoned Pork Chops with Wine Sauce

Ingredients to serve four:

4 large pork chops - leave bone in (pork steak also works well)
6 cloves garlic, minced
1 onion, minced
1/2 cup extra-virgin olive oil
4 T butter, melted
1 red sweet pepper, seeded and cut into strips
1 sweet green pepper, seeded and cut into strips
1 cup white wine (white zin works well)
2 bay leaves
3 T parsley, chopped

Rub the pork chops - both sides - with the minced garlic and onion. Sauté the chops on both sides in a heavy, non-stick skillet until well browned. Set aside and cover with foil and a towel to keep warm.

Add all other ingredients to the skillet and cook until the contents start to boil. Reduce heat to simmer. When butter has melted, discard the bay leaves. Stir the contents of the skillet until they are thoroughly blended. Place one chop on each plate and pour sauce over each.

Serve with vegetables of your choosing.

Main Dishes

Pork Steak with Wine Sauce

Ingredients to serve four:

4 half-pound pork steaks (or large chops with bones removed)
4 T extra-virgin olive oil
2 cups uncooked mushrooms, sliced
2 green onions, chopped (both white and green parts)
24 stalks asparagus, trimmed
6 basil leaves, torn or cut into narrow strips
1 cup white wine of your choosing
1/2 t each of salt and pepper

Season both sides of the steaks with salt and pepper. Sauté steaks in a large, non-stick skillet in olive oil over medium heat for about four minutes on each side. Remove and cover with foil and a towel to keep warm.

Add all other ingredients (and additional olive oil if necessary) except the wine to the skillet and cook until asparagus is tender, stirring occasionally. Add the wine to the skillet and continue cooking for another two minutes. Serve meat with wine sauce over-all.

Sausage – Bean Dinner

Ingredients to serve six:

3 pounds sweet Italian pork sausage, cut into bite-size chunks
6 tomatoes, topped, seeded and cut into wedges (bite-size)
5 cloves garlic, minced
1 onion, peeled and minced
4 T extra-virgin olive oil
juice of one lemon
2 bay leaves
1/2 cup parsley, chopped
6 basil leaves, torn or cut into narrow strips
3 - 14 1/2 oz. cns. white beans
1/2 t each salt and pepper

In a large skillet, sauté the onion a couple of minutes in the olive oil until onion is translucent. Add the garlic the second minute. Add all ingredients including the liquid from the beans (but not the beans) and cook over medium heat, stirring occasionally, for 30 minutes.

Add beans and continue to cook for another 10 minutes.

Discard the bay leaves. Serve piping hot (make sure sausages are done).

Main Dishes

Italian Sausage with Vegetables

Ingredients to serve four:

4 medium potatoes (pre-cooked; cut into one inch chunks and boiled)
1 sweet onion, broken into rings
1 fennel bulb, quartered and cut into 2 inch pieces
1 bell pepper, seeded and cut into 2 inch slices
2 pounds sweet Italian sausage links, cut into one inch chunks
1/2 cup olive oil

Pre-cook potato chunks.

Sauté all ingredients in olive oil in large skillet until hot.

Lamb or Veal Roast

Ingredients to serve four to six:

four pound roast - no bones - no fat
1/2 pound cheap bacon - the fatter the better
2 T extra-virgin olive oil
2 cloves garlic, minced
1 medium onion, peeled and chopped fine

Sauté the garlic and onion in the oil - just until the onion is translucent.

Brush all sides of the roast with the oil - garlic - onion mixture. Place the roast in an appropriate roasting pan. Pour any left-over liquid over the roast. Lay the bacon strips side by side on the top of the roast. Insert a meat thermometer in the thickest part of the roast. Bake in a pre-heated 300 degree oven, uncovered.

Check the thermometer regularly. It will be done "rare" when it reaches 150 degrees. If you like it well done, leave it in longer.

Remove the bacon and cut the roast into 1/2 inch thick slices (wider if you wish).

Pour the liquid in the bottom of the roaster into a gravy boat and invite your guests to ladle the juices over each serving.

Main Dishes

Fettuccine with Bacon Bits

Ingredients to serve four:

1 package (16 ounces) fettuccine
1 pound thick sliced bacon cut into quarter inch cubes
2 cups chopped asparagus or broccoli
2 T lemon juice
4 T olive oil
2/3 cup grated Parmesan cheese

Sauté bacon cubes - don't let burn.

Cook broccoli or asparagus in boiling water 3 or 4 minutes until tender. Remove with slotted spoon, set aside and add fettuccine to the water and cook according to directions on the package.

Drain pasta and return to pot. Add vegetable, bacon bits, lemon juice and olive oil. Gently toss. Serve on four plates or in bowls; sprinkle each serving with Parmesan.

Polenta Casserole

Or as my Iron Range Italian friends would call it: Cornmeal hotdish!

Ingredients to serve six to eight:

1 pound Italian hot sausage - remove casings
1 pound hamburger or ground pork
4 T extra-virgin olive oil
4 cloves garlic, minced
2 onions, peeled and minced
2 - 14 1/2 oz. cns. crushed tomatoes (Italian style)
1 egg plant - chunked
1 zucchini - chunked
1 cup grated cheese of your choosing (Parmesan works well)

2 cups chicken broth
4 cups water
1 1/2 cups cornmeal
1/2 t salt

In a non-stick heavy skillet, sauté the ground beef and Italian sausage in the olive oil. Add the onions and garlic the last minute - continue stirring. Add tomatoes, eggplant and zucchini and continue to cook, stirring every few minutes, until it starts to boil, then reduce heat to simmer and continue cooking another 10 minutes or until squash and eggplant are tender.

In a microwave safe dish, combine water, salt, chicken broth and cornmeal. Microwave on high until mixture is thick. Stop to stir occasionally. Remove from microwave and stir-in grated cheese. Line oven-safe casserole dish with cornmeal mixture, including sides of the dish.

Spoon sausage - tomato mixture into casserole and bake in a pre-heated 300 degree oven for 30 minutes. When serving, be sure to include some of the cornmeal.

Cauliflower with Pasta

Ingredients to serve four:

1 - 16 oz. pkg. or box ravioli or pasta of your choosing
4 cups cauliflower florets (or you may substitute asparagus tips)
2 cns. chicken broth or chicken soup with herbs
1/2 cup Parmesan cheese, grated (or other cheese of your choosing)
1/2 t salt
1/2 t black pepper

Prepare pasta according to directions on the box or package. Drain.

Place chicken broth in a sauce pan; add 2 cns. of water. Add salt and pepper. Add the cauliflower florets and cook over medium heat until tender (about 10 minutes).

Serve pasta, broth and cauliflower in bowls with grated cheese sprinkled on top.

Pizza - Option #1

The easiest way to make pizza from scratch at home us to buy pizza dough at the nearest pizza restaurant or pick it up at your favorite super market. But - in case you really want to make it totally from scratch including the crust, let's begin with this step by step procedure:

Ingredients:

3 cups bread flour, divided
1 1/2 cups warm water
1 t sugar

1 1/2 t salt
1 1/3 t active dry yeast

Step# 1

In a bowl, pour in the warm water, stir in the sugar and sprinkle the yeast on top. Stir in the yeast and then let stand about 10 minutes. Mixture will start to look "spongy".

Step #2

Stir in 2 1/2 cups of the flour and salt. Let stand until dough forms.

Step #3

Sprinkle half the remainder of the flour on a work surface and then dump the dough on that surface. Knead the dough about 10 minutes until smooth. Dust with remainder of the flour and turn into a large bowl. Cover the bowl with a dish towel. Set in a warm area (no drafts) and let rise for about 1 1/2 hours. The dough will double in volume.

Step #4

Divide the dough into four equal parts, cover with the dish towel and let sit 30 minutes.

Step #5

Using a rolling pin, roll each of the four pieces of dough into 10 inch circles. Bake the crusts in a 300 degree, pre-heated oven on a lightly oiled cookie sheet - about 3 minutes.

For topping for this first recipe, let's do something exotic - like a half dozen sliced pears and 2 cups of crushed pecans on a generous cheese spread of your choosing. Return to the oven until the cheese melts (just a few minutes).

Three Cheese Pizza

Ingredients for one pizza to serve four:

1 pound pizza dough (available in most supermarkets)
8 oz. each of three kinds of cheese of your choosing - grated (Parmesan, Fontina, Provolone,
  Mozzarella and Pecorino Romano all work well)
3 T extra-virgin olive oil
1 T each of chopped marjoram, basil, thyme and parsley
1/2 pound pepperoni, sliced extra thin

Work pizza dough into a circle roughly 1/8 inch thick (a rolling pin works well). Brush with olive oil. Bake in a pre-heated 350 degree oven on an oiled surface (metal or ceramic oven-safe pan). With the oiled surface of the pizza down, when the top surface starts to bubble or starts to turn brown on the edges, remove from the oven (after about 3 or 4 minutes).

Combine the grated cheeses and scatter them evenly over the pizza dough. Scatter the chopped herbs over the pizza. Distribute the pepperoni slices over the pizza.

Return to the oven on a lower shelf and broil on high. Watch closely and remove from the oven as soon as the cheeses melt.

Another option is to not mix the cheeses but distribute each on one-third of the dough and cut very narrow slices so each of your guests can sample each kind of cheese.

More About Pizza

The fun of making your own pizza lies in your great opportunity to be creative with your choice of toppings. In the previous two pizza recipes we talked about how the easiest way to form the crust is to buy the dough at a pizza parlor or from your local supermarket or there are some packages you can buy where you just add water. However, if you wanted to do it all from scratch we told you how in the first recipe. Below is a suggested list of toppings from which you can choose:

MEATS:

sweet Italian sausage
hot Italian sausage
pepperoni
ham
bacon
ground beef, pork or veal
some kinds of fish (like anchovies)
pieces of chicken or turkey
luncheon meats

HERBS AND SEASONINGS:

garlic
onion
basil
oregano
thyme
parsley
crushed red pepper flakes

VEGETABLES:

tomatoes
zucchini
eggplant
squash

FRUIT:

pineapple
pears
bananas (add after baking)
strawberries
jam or jelly

NUTS:

almonds - crushed
pecans - crushed
walnuts - crushed

Shrimp with an Italian Touch - #1

Ingredients:

1 1/2 pounds shrimp (larger rather than smaller), peeled
16 oz. box or package of Angel Hair spaghetti (capellini) or pasta of your choice
4 T extra-virgin olive oil
4 cloves garlic, minced
2 14-16 oz. cans crushed or diced tomatoes (Italian style)
2/3 cup sweet (dessert) wine
2 T torn or chopped basil
1/2 t each salt and pepper

Sauté the shrimp and garlic in the olive oil - turn the shrimp once - about 1 minute on each side.

Add the tomatoes, wine, salt and pepper and cook until piping hot - stirring occasionally.

Meanwhile, prepare the pasta according to the directions on the package and drain.

Divide the pasta onto four plates. Top with sauce. Scatter basil over each serving for garnish.

Spaghetti with Shrimp - #2

Ingredients to serve four:

1 - 16 oz. box spaghetti or other favorite pasta
1 pound (or more) fresh (or thawed if frozen) shrimp - shelled and de-veined
1 - 28 oz. cn. tomatoes, crushed or chopped - preferably Italian style
3 cloves garlic, minced
1/2 t black pepper

In a skillet, stir together and cook tomatoes, garlic and pepper. After two or three minutes, add shrimp and continue cooking until shrimp are opaque throughout. (About 3 minutes)

Meanwhile, bring a pot of water to boiling and then cook spaghetti according to directions on the package. Drain spaghetti when done and then return to the pot and add tomato-shrimp mixture - stirring all the while.

Serve on four plates.

Optional: 1 or 2 cups fresh, chopped basil leaves

Main Dishes

Capellini with Shrimp – Recipe #3

Ingredients to serve four:

1 - 16 oz. pkg. capellini (or other pasta or your choosing)
32 medium size shrimp, peeled and deveined
4 T extra-virgin olive oil
4 cloves garlic, minced
2 cns. crushed or diced tomatoes - Italian style
2 T capers
1/3 cup white wine
4 T basil, cut into strips
4 T parsley, chopped
1 /4 t red pepper flakes
1/2 t salt
1/2 cup shredded Parmesan cheese

Cook capellini according to directions on the package. Add olive oil to skillet and sauté garlic and pepper flakes a couple of minutes or until garlic changes color. Add shrimp and continue to cook a couple of minutes, turning shrimp at least once.

Add tomatoes, capers, wine and salt. Bring to a boil, then reduce heat and let simmer five or six minutes, stirring occasionally. Drain cooked pasta and add to the skillet. Continue to simmer, stirring occasionally, until sure all ingredients are hot.

Transfer to four dinner plates and sprinkle with Parmesan, parsley and basil.

Shrimp with Angel Hair Pasta and Herbs - #4

Ingredients to serve four to six:

1 pound angel hair pasta (or pasta of your choosing)
2 - 14 1/2 oz. cns. crushed tomatoes, Italian style
4 T basil, cut or torn into small pieces
4 green onions, chopped, both green and white parts
1/2 t crushed red pepper flakes
1 pound shrimp, deveined and peeled
3 cloves garlic, minced
4 T extra-virgin olive oil

Prepare pasta according to directions on the package.

Meanwhile, in a large skillet, sauté the green onions and garlic in the olive oil (onions for two minutes; garlic for one minute).

Add the tomatoes, shrimp, basil and pepper flakes to the skillet. Heat (and stir) until it starts to boil. Drain pasta and combine with the contents of the skillet. Serve hot.

Main Dishes

Linguini with Shrimp, Scallops and Crab Meat*

Ingredients to serve four:

16 oz. pkg. linguini or other favorite pasta
16 shrimp (more if small, fewer if large)
16 scallops (more if small, fewer if large)
10 oz. cn. crabmeat
10 oz. cn. mushrooms, sliced and drained
1/4 cup extra-virgin olive oil
4 green onions, chopped, both white and green parts
1/2 stick butter, melted

Sauce ingredients:

2 T olive oil
1/2 stick butter, melted
3 cloves garlic, minced
1/2 t each salt and pepper
1 onion, chopped
2 cups heavy cream
2 cups white wine
1/2 cup clam juice
1/2 t red pepper flakes

Prepare sauce in a heavy, non-stick frying pan. Melt butter and add olive oil. Sauté onion for two minutes and then add garlic and continue for one minute. Add wine and continue to cook, reducing sauce to about 1/3 original volume. Add cream and clam juice. Bring to a boil; remove from heat. Stir in seasonings. Set aside. Prepare pasta according to directions on the package.

Meanwhile, in the same pan as used to make the sauce, sauté (in butter and olive oil) the shrimp and scallops; toss or gently stir - about 6 minutes. Add sauce and crab meat and continue to cook until seafood is done. Garnish with chopped green onions. Additional garnish can be provided by adding grated cheese of your choice (Parmesan works well). Combine with the pasta - gently toss.

Garnish with chopped green onions. Additional garnish may be provided by adding grated cheese of your choice (Parmesan works well).

*Courtesy Jerry Mevissen, Sebeka, MN

Baked Bass Fillets

Most any white-meated fish will work well.

Ingredients to serve four:

4 fillets, about 1/2 pound each - skinned and deboned
2 lemons - juice from one and slices from the other
1 orange, peeled, seeded and cut into half-inch cubes
3 T butter, melted
1/2 cup black olives, pitted and sliced
1 small cn. mushrooms, sliced
4 T chopped pecans
2 cloves garlic, minced
salt and pepper

Lay the fillets in a greased baking dish. Combine lemon juice and melted butter and brush over fillets. Sprinkle lightly with salt and pepper.

Bake in a pre-heated 400 degree oven about 15 minutes or until fillets flake easily with a fork.

In the meantime, combine olives, mushrooms, pecans, orange chunks and garlic. Scatter this mixture over the baked fillets. Scatter lemon slices over the fillets.

Serve hot.

Main Dishes

Baked Bass with Tomatoes and Herbs

Ingredients to serve four:

4 half-pound fillets, skinned and de-boned (most any fish may be substituted)
3 T extra-virgin olive oil
juice of one lemon
4 T basil leaves, chopped
1/2 t each salt and pepper
2 large, ripe tomatoes, topped and sliced about a quarter inch thick
4 T Parmesan cheese (or cheese of your choosing) grated

Combine olive oil, lemon juice, salt and pepper. Cover the bottom of a flat baking dish with this mixture. Lay fillets side by side in the oil mixture and then turn them over. Top the fillets with the chopped basil, then tomato slices and, lastly, with the Parmesan cheese.

Bake in a pre-heated, 400 degree oven for ten minutes or until thick end of the fillet flakes easily with a fork.

Bass with Tomato Sauce

First generation Italian Americans no doubt missed the fish from the Mediterranean but many more than made up for it by enjoying fish from Minnesota's fresh waters with traditional Italian recipes.

Ingredients to serve four:

2 pounds bass fillets, skinned and de-boned
2 - 14 1/2 oz. cns. crushed tomatoes (preferably Italian style)
1/2 cup basil leaves - torn
2 T capers
1 T lemon zest, grated
juice of 1 lemon
1/2 t each of salt and pepper

Combine the bottom six ingredients.

Line a baking dish or pan with foil. Pour half the sauce onto the foil. Cut the fillets into four equal pieces and lay on top of the sauce in the pan. Ladle the rest of the sauce over the fillets. Cover with another sheet of foil. Bake in a 350 degree oven until the fillet flakes easily with a fork - about one hour.

Serve with side dishes of your choosing.

Main Dishes

Lemon Stuffed Fish

Ingredients to serve six:

1/2 cup finely chopped celery
1/4 cup chopped onion
2 cloves garlic, minced
3 tablespoons butter
4 cups dry bread cubes or croutons
1/2 tsp. grated lemon peel
4 tsp. lemon juice
1 tablespoon snipped parsley
2 tablespoons torn basil
1 tablespoon butter, melted

Place 2 fillets in a greased baking pan. Cook celery, garlic, and onion in 3 tablespoons butter until crisp tender. Pour over bread. Add lemon peel and juice, parsley, 1/2 tsp. salt and a dash of pepper, and toss together. Spoon half the stuffing mixture on each fillet in the pan.

Top with remaining two pieces of fish, brush with 1 tablespoon butter. Sprinkle with salt and paprika and bake, covered at 350 degrees for about 25 minutes.

Iron Range Baked Northern with Raisin Stuffing

This recipe works equally well with muskies, bass or whitefish. Northerns should weigh four pounds or more, whitefish at least three.

Stuffing Ingredients:

1 cup raisins
1/4 lb. butter (melted in one cup hot water)
2 cups croutons or dry bread crumbs
1 large onion, chopped but not too fine
salt and pepper
1 cup chopped bologna (or wieners or polish sausage or luncheon meat)
   (I don't think this part of the recipe came from Italy!)

Preparing the fish: Scale and gut the fish; remove the head, tail and all fins. Wash and dry the fish, inside and out. Score the back of the fish with cross-section cuts about three inches apart — down to the backbone. Salt and pepper, inside and out and in the cuts.

Place the croutons, raisins, meat and onions in a bowl. Salt and pepper lightly while stirring the ingredients together. Add and stir in the butter-hot water mixture just before stuffing the fish. Lay a sheet of foil on the bottom of the roaster. Stuff the fish (loosely) and place upright on the sheet of foil. Fold the foil up along both sides of the fish — do not cover the back. The foil will hold in the stuffing. If your fish is too long for the roaster, you may cut it in two and bake the two sections side by side. Leftover stuffing or additional stuffing may be baked in a foil package alongside the fish or even outside the roaster. Place a strip of bacon and a slice of onion, alternately, over each score (or cut). Cover the roaster and place in a preheated, 300 degree oven. After one hour, remove cover and continue to bake until the meat becomes flaky and separates easily from the backbone (as viewed from the end of the fish). This should take about another half-hour, depending on the size of the fish. Transfer the baked fish to a platter. Cut through the backbone at each score mark, separating the fish into serving-size portions. The stuffing may be lifted out with each portion as it is served. Serve with tartar sauce and/or lemon.

Fish Fillets with Tomato Sauce

Ingredients to serve four:

2 pounds fish fillets
2 - 14 1/2 oz. cans crushed tomatoes (Italian Style)
2 tablespoons extra-virgin olive oil
2 T Italian salad dressing mix
1/2 tsp. salt
1 cup grated Parmesan cheese

Place fish in a greased shallow baking pan. Combine tomato sauce, salad oil, dressing mix and salt. Pour sauce over fish. Sprinkle with Parmesan cheese. Bake at 350° for about 40 minutes until fish flakes easily.

Fresh Fish Stuffed with Seafood

Ingredients to serve six:

2 cups cooked chopped shrimp or crabmeat
3 to 4 pounds de-boned fillets
2 eggs
1 cup cream
2 tablespoons butter
1 cup chopped canned or fresh mushrooms
2 T chopped chives
1 tablespoon flour
salt and paprika
4 tablespoons sherry
2 limes or lemons

Mix the shrimp, egg and 1/2 cup of the cream together. Melt butter, add mushrooms and chives and sauté until soft, add flour and cook. Add shrimp mixture and cook until thick.

Place fish in a buttered baking dish and spread the mixture between the two sides of the fish. Pour over the remaining cream, sprinkle with salt and paprika. Add sherry (optional) and bake at 350° for 45 minutes.

Serve with fresh lime quarters or lemons.

Main Dishes

Cheesy Perch

Ingredients to serve four:

1 1/2 pounds perch fillets
1 1/2 cups cheesy cracker crumbs (like "Cheezits" or other cheese flavored crackers)
1 cup corn meal
1/2 cup flour
1 egg
2 cups water
1/2 t each salt and pepper
1/2 cup extra-virgin olive oil

Make fine crumbs out of the crackers, either with a rolling pin or food processor. Combine the cracker crumbs, corn meal, flour, salt and pepper.

Pour the water into a small bowl; break an egg into it and beat with a fork until smooth. Dip each fillet into the egg-water mixture and then coat both sides in the cracker crumb - corn meal - flour mixture.

Pour the olive oil into a large skillet. Pre-heat over medium-hot and then fry the fillets on both sides - turning once.

Linguine and Halibut

Ingredients to serve four:

1 box or pkg. (16 oz.) Linguine
2 pounds halibut fillets, cut bite size
4 T extra-virgin olive oil
3 garlic cloves, minced
1 large onion, chopped
1 cn. diced or crushed tomatoes (preferably Italian style)
salt and pepper
1/3 cup chopped parsley
1/3 cup basil leaves cut in strips

Prepare linguini according to directions on package. Place halibut chunks in a sauce pan and cover with about an inch of water to which 2 T salt and 2 T sugar have been added. Poach fish; the chunks will come to the surface when done.

Set halibut aside. Discard water and add olive oil to the pan and sauté onion and garlic a couple of minutes or until onion is translucent and garlic is brown. Add tomatoes, halibut and linguini and continue to heat, stirring gently all the while.

When thoroughly warm, transfer to a platter and sprinkle with parsley and basil strips.

Main Dishes

Salted Codfish in a Skillet

Here is another example of people celebrating a holiday by going back to earlier, poorer times - in this case, when fish was preserved by drying.

Ingredients to serve eight:

4 pounds of salted cod, soaked in cold water 48 hours (fresh cod may be substituted)

1 large onions, chopped

1 cup all purpose flour, seasoned with 1/4 t salt and 1/2 t white pepper

1 1/2 cups green olives, pitted and sliced

1/2 cup chopped parsley

1/2 cup olive oil

2 lemons, quartered

Sauté onion in heavy skillet in a little oil until translucent; do not burn. Remove onions. Add balance of oil to skillet.

Drain cod; pat dry. Cut into serving size pieces. Dredge cod in flour seasoned with salt and pepper. Fry in olive oil until brown on both sides. As cod is fried, place on a platter. When all fish have been fried and removed from skillet, add olives, onion and parsley to the skillet.

Return cod to the skillet a few pieces at a time, turning and coating with mixture (just for a couple of minutes). Spoon leftover juices and olives in the skillet over the fish - on a platter.

Serve with lemon wedges.

Pasta with Tuna

Italian immigrants must have missed enjoying the varieties of fish from the bountiful Mediterranean. The canned tuna available even in the comer grocery store was a handy and tasty replacement.

Ingredients to serve four:

1 - 16 oz. box or package of pasta of your choosing

3 - 14 1/2 oz. cns. crushed or diced tomatoes (preferably Italian style)

2 - 6-8 oz. cns. tunafish

1 T torn or cut basil

1 T chopped parsley

2 T capers (drained)

1 T lemon juice

1/2 t each salt and pepper

1/2 t red pepper flakes

Cut the tuna (drained) into bite-size chunks. Place all the ingredients (except the pasta) in a sauce pan and cook until piping hot.

Meanwhile, prepare the pasta according to directions on the package. Drain, but add 1 cup of the liquid to the sauce.

Combine the sauce and the pasta.

Main Dishes

Pasta with Clams

Here's a great recipe - providing you can find a seafood market in your town!

Ingredients to serve four:

1 - 16 oz. box or package of spaghetti or other pasta of your choosing
2 - 14 1/2 oz. cans crushed or diced tomatoes (preferably Italian)
36 clams
4 garlic cloves, minced
1 onion, minced
4 T extra-virgin olive oil
3 T sugar
1/2 T red pepper flakes

Sauté the garlic and onion in the olive oil until onions are translucent and garlic starts to turn brown.

Add the tomatoes, sugar and red pepper flakes to the skillet and cook until piping hot (10-12 minutes). Add the clams and continue cooking until clams are wide open. Discard any clams that have not opened after 10 minutes.

Meanwhile, cook the pasta according to the directions on the package and drain. Distribute the pasta to four plates and then add equal portions of sauce and clams.

Clams, Stuffed and Baked

Ingredients to serve four:

24 clams

Ingredients for topping:

1 cup bread crumbs
1/4 cup extra-virgin olive oil
2 cloves garlic - minced
1/3 cup grated cheese of your choosing
1/3 t oregano
1/3 t salt
1/2 cup water in which clams were boiled

Boil clams in water until open wide (throw away any unopened clams). Remove clams from water (use a slotted spoon) and let cool.

Place half shells with meat attached on a cookie sheet. Combine topping ingredients and sprinkle over clams. Bake in 350 degree pre-heated oven until crumbs are golden brown.

Main Dishes

CHAPTER VI

DESSERTS

Cheese Pudding with Grapes

Ingredients to serve six - eight:

1 pound ricotta or other soft cheese
3 T butter, melted
3 eggs
2 T bread crumbs
6 T sugar
1/2 t cinnamon
4 T crushed walnuts or pecans (toasted optional)
3 cups grapes - seedless (your choice of color)
2 T wine vinegar
1/2 t salt

Brush some of the butter on the inside of a 10 inch pie plate. Coat inside of pie plate with bread crumbs.

Using a blender, combine the cheese, eggs, salt, cinnamon and half the sugar. Blend until smooth. Pour mixture into pie plate. Sprinkle surface with crushed nuts. Bake in a pre-heated 375 degree oven for 25 minutes or until golden.

In the meantime, combine the remainder of the sugar and melted butter and wine vinegar in a baking dish and toss grapes (may be halved - your choice) until well coated. After removing pudding from oven to let cool, bake grapes 10 minutes - shaking a few times.

When grapes have cooled, serve with pudding.

Oranges in Custard Sauce

Ingredients to serve eight:

10 navel oranges (remove peel and pith and cut into thin cross-sections)
1 1/2 cups sugar
3/4 cup water
1/4 t lemon juice

Custard sauce:

4 eggs, yolk only
1/4 cup sugar
4 T flour, all-purpose
1 cup milk
1 t vanilla
2 T liqueur (maraschino if available)

Cut oranges and set aside. Make a syrup by boiling the sugar and lemon juice in the water. Boil until the sugar is dissolved and the liquid becomes syrupy.

Beat together the egg yolk and sugar; add flour; stir together. Meanwhile, heat milk to boiling point, but do not let boil. Add hot milk to egg mixture. Cook over low heat, stirring all the while until it thickens. Do not boil. Stir in the liqueur and vanilla.

Chill oranges and custard sauce for at least 8 hours. Pour custard over oranges when served.

Cream Cake

This one is a little work, but it's worth the effort.

Ingredients:

for cake:

2 cups heavy cream
6 eggs, separated
1 t baking soda
1/2 stick butter, softened
2 cups sugar
1/2 cup extra-virgin olive oil
2 cups flour (all purpose)
1 t vanilla extract

for frosting:

1 pound cream cheese, softened
3 cups confectioners sugar
6 T butter, softened
1 1/2 t vanilla extract
1 cup chopped walnuts (or nuts of your choice)

Lightly grease 3 - 10 inch cake pans. Beat egg whites until stiff. Combine with cream and baking soda.

Combine sugar (granulated), butter and oil in a mixer. Add egg yolks one at a time, mixing them in thoroughly. Add cream mixture and flour, alternately. Stir in vanilla and egg whites Pour into 3 pans. Bake 30 minutes in a pre-heated 300 degree oven. A wood toothpick inserted in middle will come out clean if done. Let pans cool on a wire rack 15 minutes, then turn cakes out of pans on rack. Let cool.

Prepare frosting by combining cream cheese and butter (beat until smooth). Still using the mixer, blend in confectioners' sugar and vanilla. Spread frosting between layers and on top and sides of the cake. Scatter with nuts. Refrigerate.

Cheesecake with a Touch of Chocolate

Ingredients for 1 cheesecake 8 - 12 servings:

24 - 28 ounces vanilla wafers
32 - 36 ounces cream cheese (softened)
8 t cocoa or other chocolate powder
1 cup sugar
1 cup sour cream
4 eggs, beaten
2 cups whipping cream
4 T hot water

In a lightly greased pie tin or baking dish, make a layer of vanilla wafers. In half the hot water, dissolve half the cocoa and spread over the wafers. Make a second layer of wafers and dissolve the rest of the cocoa in the rest of the hot water and spread over this second layer.

Combine the cream cheese, sour cream, sugar and eggs with a mixer - at slow speed. Spread this mixture over the layers of wafers. Bake in a 300 degree oven for one hour. Refrigerate over-night.

Beat whipping cream until stiff and spread over cheesecake before serving.

Desserts

Cheesecake #2

Ingredients to serve eight:

Crust:

1 cup graham cracker crumbs
1/2 stick butter, melted
4 T brown sugar

Ingredients for filling:

16 oz. cream cheese - softened (You may use more than one variety of cheese)
4 eggs, beaten
1 cup sugar
1 T vanilla extract

Topping ingredients:

whipped cream or an envelope of topping mix

Combine crust ingredients and press onto the bottom of a lightly greased pie tin or oval baking dish. Bake 15 minutes in a pre-heated 300 degree oven. Let cool.

Combine the filling ingredients in a mixing bowl at low speed. Pour over crust. Bake one hour in a pre-heated 300 degree oven. Let cool. Then run a knife around the edges. Refrigerate at least two hours, then top with whipped cream or prepare topping mix according to directions on the package.

Option: Mince a chocolate bar or sprinkle powder from a chocolate drink - like cocoa - over topping.

Italian Cheesecake - #3

It should come as no surprise that Italians have a great recipe for cheesecake.

Ingredients:

Filling:

1 - 8 oz. package cream cheese - softened
36 oz. ricotta cheese
4 T flour
1 cup sugar
juice of 1 lemon
1 t vanilla extract
4 large eggs

Crust ingredients:

1 1/2 cups graham cracker crumbs
1/8 lb. (1/2 stick) butter, melted
4 T sugar

Combine crust ingredients and press onto bottom and sides of a 9 inch pie tin. Bake in a pre-heated 350 degree oven for ten minutes. Let cool before filling.

Combine all filling ingredients in a large bowl. An electric mixer works best. Fill crust and bake in a pre-heated 350 degree oven for one hour.

Cool and then refrigerate before serving.

Desserts

Other Books by Dr. Duane R. Lund

A Beginner's Guide to Hunting and Trapping
A Kid's Guidebook to Fishing Secrets
Fishing and Hunting Stories from The Lake of the Woods
Andrew, Youngest Lumberjack
The Youngest Voyageur
White Indian Boy
Gull Lake, Yesterday and Today
Lake of the Woods, Yesterday and Today, Vol. 1
Lake of the Woods, Earliest Accounts, Vol. 2
Lake of the Woods (The Last 50 Years and the Next)
Leech Lake, Yesterday and Today
The North Shore of Lake Superior, Yesterday and Today
Our Historic Boundary Waters
Our Historic Upper Mississippi
Tales of Four Lakes and a River
The Indian Wars
Chief Flatmouth
101 Favorite Freshwater Fish Recipes
101 Favorite Wild Rice Recipes
101 Favorite Mushroom Recipes
150 Ways to Enjoy Potatoes

Early Native American Recipes and Remedies
Camp Cooking, Made Easy and Fun
The Scandinavian Cookbook
Cooking Minnesotan, yoo-betcha!
More than 50 Ways to enjoy Lefse
Entertainment Helpers, Quick and Easy
Gourmet Freshwater Fish Recipes
Nature's Bounty for Your Table
Sauces, Seasonings and Marinades for
   Fish and Wild Game
The Soup Cookbook
Traditional Holiday Ethnic Recipes -
   collected all over the world
The Life And Times of THREE POWERFUL
   OJIBWA CHIEFS *Curly Head Hole-In-The-Day the elder,
   Hole-In-The-Day the younger*
Hasty But Tasty
Fruit & Nut Recipes
Europeans In North America *Before Columbus*
Hunting and Fishing in Alaska
German Home Cooking

ABOUT THE AUTHOR

- EDUCATOR (RETIRED, SUPERINTENDENT OF SCHOOLS, STAPLES, MINNESOTA);
- HISTORIAN (PAST MEMBER OF EXECUTIVE BOARD, MINNESOTA HISTORICAL SOCIETY);
  Past Member of BWCA and National Wilderness Trails Advisory Committees;
- SENIOR CONSULTANT to the Blandin Foundation
- WILDLIFE ARTIST, OUTDOORSMAN.